AF809188

China's Private Army

Alessandro Arduino

China's Private Army

Protecting the New Silk Road

palgrave
macmillan

Alessandro Arduino
Co-Director Security & Crisis Management Program
Shanghai Academy of Social Sciences—UNITO
Shanghai, China

ISBN 978-981-10-7214-7 ISBN 978-981-10-7215-4 (eBook)
https://doi.org/10.1007/978-981-10-7215-4

Library of Congress Control Number: 2017963548

© The Editor(s) (if applicable) and The Author(s) 2018
This work is subject to copyright. All rights are solely and exclusively licensed by the Publisher, whether the whole or part of the material is concerned, specifically the rights of translation, reprinting, reuse of illustrations, recitation, broadcasting, reproduction on microfilms or in any other physical way, and transmission or information storage and retrieval, electronic adaptation, computer software, or by similar or dissimilar methodology now known or hereafter developed.
The use of general descriptive names, registered names, trademarks, service marks, etc. in this publication does not imply, even in the absence of a specific statement, that such names are exempt from the relevant protective laws and regulations and therefore free for general use.
The publisher, the authors and the editors are safe to assume that the advice and information in this book are believed to be true and accurate at the date of publication. Neither the publisher nor the authors or the editors give a warranty, express or implied, with respect to the material contained herein or for any errors or omissions that may have been made. The publisher remains neutral with regard to jurisdictional claims in published maps and institutional affiliations.

Cover illustration: Abstract Bricks and Shadows © Stephen Bonk/Fotolia.co.uk

Printed on acid-free paper

This Palgrave Pivot imprint is published by Springer Nature
The registered company is Springer Nature Singapore Pte Ltd.
The registered company address is: 152 Beach Road, #21-01/04 Gateway East, Singapore 189721, Singapore

This book is dedicated to Gian Matteo with the hope that
he will always be able to find his moral compass
in any uncharted territory.

Acknowledgements

The core insights of this volume are based on interviews and workshops that were carried out in China and along the Belt and Road. I would like to extend my personal thanks to many people who devoted their precious time to shed light on the privatization of the Chinese state's monopoly of force. Some experts and practitioners prefer to be anonymous, but I want you to know that without your support and knowledge I could not have accomplished this task.

I am indebted to many friends and colleagues and would like to acknowledge the intellectual support of Dr Paul Cole in challenging, more often bluntly than not, my early drafts; Prof. Li Yihai for supporting my quest; Prof. Li Mingjiang for believing in a future for Chinese Private Security research; and Dr James Dorsey for his sharp critique and for pointing me towards new sources of information. Raffaello, Jianming, Yaniv, Mick, Kerry, Christian, Randy, Dexi, Jacob, Yu, James, Zhao, Joey, Andrew, Huang, Mike and Pat—you know.

A deeply heartfelt thank you goes to all the supportive colleagues from Shanghai Academy of Social Sciences, S. Rajaratnam School of International Studies, as well as the University of Turin.

Last but not the least, I would like to express my gratitude to my editor Mr Jacob Dreyer for graciously tolerating my rants and to Ms Anushangi Weerakoon for her kind support.

Contents

List of Abbreviations

AIIB	Asian Infrastructure Investment Bank
ANA	Afghan National Army
AVIC	Aviation Industry Corporation of China
BRI	Belt and Road Initiative
CIRC	China Insurance Regulatory Commission
CMC	Central Military Commission
CPEC	China Pakistan Economic Corridor
CSR	Corporate Social Responsibilities
CSSC	China State Shipbuilding Corporation
CSTO	Collective Security Treaty Organization
EEU	Eurasian Economic Union
FDI	Foreign Direct Investment
FSG	Frontier Service Group
G2G	Government-to-Government
ICoCA	International Code of Conduct Association
IS	Islamic State
K&R	Kidnapping and Ransom
M&A	Merger and Acquisition
MFA	Ministry of Foreign Affairs
MIC	Military Industrial Complex
MOFCOM	Ministry of Commerce
NDN	Northern Distribution Network
NDRC	National Development and Reform Commission
NPM	New Public Management
NRA	National Revolutionary Army

NSA	Non-state Actor
OBOR	One Belt One Road
ODI	Outbound Direct Investment
PAP	People's Armed Police
PLA	People's Liberation Army
PLAN	People's Liberation Army's Navy
PMF	Private Military Firm
PMSC	Private Military Security Companies
PSC	Private Security Companies
RATS	Regional Anti-terrorist Structure
RFP	Requests for Proposal
SASAC	State-Owned Assets Supervision and Administration Commission
SASS	Shanghai Academy of Social Sciences
SCO	Shanghai Cooperation Organization
SIGIR	Special Inspector General for Iraqi Reconstruction
SIIS	Shanghai Institute for International Studies
SOE	State-Owned Enterprise
SRA	Sindhudesh Revolutionary Army
WTO	World Trade Organization

CHAPTER 1

Protecting the New Silk Road

Abstract The Belt and Road Initiative (BRI) launched by President Xi Jinping in 2013, which is intended to promote economic development and exchanges between China and more than 60 countries, is gaining momentum. The BRI is not immune, however, to a number of important risks that in many instances are new to Chinese companies operating abroad. One oversight that must be addressed is that the BRI requires a wide range of security considerations along both the maritime and land routes. While the security problem has not gone unnoticed in Beijing, the solutions could be found elsewhere, namely in international companies that provide armed private security, special risk assessment, insurance and, perhaps most importantly, crisis mitigation.

Keywords Belt and Road Initiative • Private security company • OBOR • BRI security • China risk

1.1 Introduction

On May 31, 2016 the Sindhudesh Revolutionary Army (SRA), a little-known local group which directly challenges the Pakistani central government's control over of the Sindh province, made an attempt on the life of Chinese workers based in the Pakistani city of Karachi. The attack, made with an improvised explosive device, injured a Chinese engineer and his

© The Author(s) 2018

A. Arduino, *China's Private Army*,
https://doi.org/10.1007/978-981-10-7215-4_1

> driver. In early 2016 three Chinese executives of the China Railway Corp were killed along with other foreigners in the terrorist attack at the Blue Radisson hotel in Bamako, Mali's capital.

Both groups of Chinese had neither adequate protection nor an appropriate forewarning of the imminent threats in the area. In the case of the Bamako terror attack, the Chinese became a target of opportunity for no other reason than that they were foreigners. In the Sindhudesh Revolutionary Army (SRA) attack, the Chinese workers were the designated target in order to dissuade further Chinese economic support for Pakistan's weakening economy. Beijing's backing for Islamabad has already fomented open opposition in the Baluci tribal region. However, the port city of Karachi was considered a relatively safe area for the enclave of China's workers. The China Pakistan Economic Corridor, with an estimated investment value of US$63 billion from China, is a strategic part of the Belt and Road Initiative (BRI) that connects Central Asia to the Indian Ocean port of Gwadar in Pakistan. The BRI, launched by President Xi Jinping in 2013, is intended to promote economic development and exchanges between China and over 60 countries. The BRI is the spearhead of renewed Chinese outbound direct investment (ODI) efforts.

Confrontations between the local population and Chinese workers are not new in Africa and Central and South Asia as disputes over working conditions and environmental degradation issues are a growing concern over China's ODI. While the volume of Chinese overseas investment has increased eightfold in the last decade, the amount of Chinese funds dedicated to the BRI is unprecedented, with a Chinese estimate of US$8 trillion.

One oversight that must be addressed is that the BRI requires a wide range of security considerations along both the maritime and land routes. In the Karachi attack, the global reach of the BRI encountered a local problem that has not been given sufficient attention during the project's economic and security impact analysis. What has been missing is an assessment of the local communities' opposition to the BRI. According to an official press release, in the incident the attackers left a note that said that this was a protest against the 'rise of Chinese imperialism'. The communiqué presents a propaganda clash against the BRI's idea of win-win sustainable development. Since the launch of the BRI in 2013, China's public diplomacy, utilizing the metaphor of the New Silk Road Global connectivity and win-win sustainable development, has attempted to manage or mitigate anxiety over what is characterized as 'China's rise'. This effort, which has not been successful, could be the harbinger of several other conflicts along the BRI route.

While the security problem has not gone unnoticed in Beijing, the solutions could be found elsewhere, namely in international companies that provide armed private security, special risk assessment, insurance and, perhaps most importantly, crisis mitigation.

The contemporary role of private security companies (PSCs) with 'Chinese characteristics' is entirely different from the role played by private military security companies (PMSCs) that were employed during the two Iraqi conflicts and the Afghan stabilization campaign. Nevertheless, Chinese state-owned enterprises (SOEs) that deploy PSCs still struggle with several perception gaps with regard to present security threats as well as how best to utilize security contractors. Most of the SOEs and private Chinese companies that are building infrastructure along the BRI tend to underestimate the risks, hoping that protection will be provided by the agreements that Beijing has inked with the host countries. Other companies that are aware of the threats tend to view PSCs as little more than 'guns for hire'.

Contemporary PSCs are making efforts to differentiate and distance their business model from the shameful acts perpetrated by mercenaries during Africa's postcolonial wars. Nonetheless, the stigma related to soldiers of fortunes is still alive.

During the past two decades, the demise of the bipolar global order has ignited the rise of private corporations that offer military-style services as part of their core business model. The modern mercenaries became contractors, offering their services through social media, including Facebook. In this respect, Chinese requirements for private security call for a more complex set of solutions. Chinese SOEs require a set of integrated services in which armed personnel are just one component.

After the killing of 17 Iraqi civilians in Nisour Square in Baghdad, the actions of the American PSC Blackwater, also labelled PMSC, generated a media outcry against the employment of private security contractors. The immediate fallout forced Blackwater's CEO Eric Prince to abandon the US government's lucrative contracts. In stark contrast to Western perceptions, a significant section of the Chinese security apparatus and PSC management perceive the Blackwater model as efficient. Mr Eric Prince's sales pitch for his former company Blackwater, which claims 'no client died during Blackwater's watch', has found fertile ground in China.

Therefore, it is no surprise that Mr Prince's newly established corporation in Hong Kong, Frontier Service Group, has an office in Beijing. In addition, he was one of the few foreign guests of honour who were invited to the Chinese 2016 PSC Association annual meeting.

An important problem, however, is that the laws in several countries that receive Chinese ODI do not permit the use of armed foreign PSCs. To compensate for this, risk assessment officers that cooperate with the Chinese corporations and local law enforcement could provide significant support. Meanwhile, Chinese insurance companies that are just entering the special insurance market must improve their operational capabilities to levels consistent with international best practices. Special insurance is a lesser-known niche market, but due to the expansion of Chinese ODI, this is already proving to be a highly profitable sector. Leading Chinese insurances companies such as Ping An and China Taiping are already extending feelers that seek cooperation with British and other international insurance experts.

Chinese corporations acknowledge that the risks associated with ODI in emerging economies include a higher failure rate due to intertwined factors such as economic crises, conflict, civil unrest, assets nationalization and currency devaluation. At the same time, the Chinese SOEs, due to their public nature with commercial capacity, have the tendency to blur the lines between commercial and political factors. Consequently, they tend to rely too optimistically on Beijing's support in case of a crisis.

The security threats to the Chinese workers in Pakistan were known in Beijing, but previous risk analyses concentrated on the bellicose factions seeking independence in the Baluchistan area. Islamabad has already deployed a considerable military force to protect Chinese nationals in that region. The attack in the Sindh area reflects the lack of a comprehensive, ongoing risk assessment as the project rolled out. While an initial risk analysis is mandatory during the pre-project assessment, it is also imperative to monitor how the ongoing project is affecting local communities.

Separatism and insurgency are primary variables in the risk assessment equation, but their value is often overestimated without taking into account local problems ignited by the influx of Chinese capitals and workers. The impact of Chinese infrastructure projects in local communities disrupts the internal dynamics of power and wealth, creating a new breed of winners and losers as well as provoking the danger of anti-Chinese sentiments. Several cases, from Central Asia to Africa and from Vietnam to Indonesia, have already showcased how the changes stimulated in the local communities by Chinese investments have ended in violent confrontations.

The number of crises that the Chinese SOEs face operating along the BRI land route's new railway lines linking China to Europe via Central Asia is increasing. Threats range from regional political and social instability, such as the border clashes between Tajikistan and Kyrgyzstan or the Kyrgyz ethnic violence in Osh (2010), to the increasing protest and acts of violence that erupted between Chinese SOE workers and the local populations such as the incident at Aktogay copper mine (Kazakhstan, 2015).

The BRI approach to crisis management is rooted in the government-to-government (G2G) agreements. This bilateral approach provides a risk assessment that is legally binding between China and the countries involved in the BRI. Nevertheless, the G2G approach is encumbered by several limitations. The most obvious is the separatists' antagonism towards their central government. Other limitations include weak links between central and provincial governments, cultural and religious barriers as well as historically rooted unresolved disputes. Due to these challenges, the ability of Chinese PSCs to provide accurate, ongoing security assessments, scenario planning, crisis prevention and mitigation is going to be a key requirement for the success in a long-term international economic cooperation and sustainable development that is at the core of the BRI.

Since 2014 the People's Public Security University in Beijing has offered a dedicated training course for counter-terrorist officials. In addition, private security training facilities have mushroomed in Beijing. With the support of British and Israeli experts, private firms train Chinese private security officers who are going to operate abroad, but the initiatives are still a drop in the ocean compared to the present needs. The rising number of Chinese PSCs deployed abroad underlines the novelty of the phenomenon and highlights the current lack of a leading Chinese corporation in the security field. Since the beginning of the new millennium, several Chinese firms have evolved their business model from a local security provider—the so-called bodyguards for wealthy clients—to international operations with liaison offices in Beijing.

Several Chinese PSCs that have emerged onto the international arena employ a mix of local and foreign resources. The number of local Chinese security companies that offer close personnel protection and unarmed guards total more than 5200 registered entities that account for roughly three million security officers. Among these companies, less than 30 have the capabilities and the experience to provide stand-alone international services (e.g., Huawei Security, VSS, Chinese Security ZGAB, Dewei and Ding Tay An Yuan). At the same time, the growing need for protective services by Chinese enterprises has attracted a large number of international players looking for cooperation with the emergent local PSCs (e.g., Control Risks, G4S, and Prosegur). Thus, the Chinese PSC capabilities in providing overseas security services are not comparable to those provided by their top foreign counterparts. Chinese SOEs, however, still preferred to employ Chinese contractors. The cooperation with international PSCs is deemed a 'necessary evil' until the Chinese PSCs acquire the skill sets required to reach high-level operational capabilities. The desire to employ only Chinese PSC is rooted not only in the required language and cultural sensitivity, but also in the opinion that only Chinese security corporations will be able to preserve the SOEs' confidential information. PSCs with 'Chinese characteristics' employ former People's Liberation Army (PLA) personnel, People's Armed Police (PAP) or Chinese security officers with links with the national security apparatus. Hence, the perception that only local PSCs are able to protect the integrity of the SOEs' business data.

The ability of Chinese enterprises to acquire funds from Chinese investment banks to invest abroad is not equally matched by the ability to produce accurate, ongoing risk assessments and contingency planning. With the exception of the Chinese oil and gas sector, there is a dangerous lack of interest among Chinese SOEs in understanding security. The fact that Chinese corporations still do not differentiate anti-Chinese violence from political and criminal activity is an obvious example.

Currently most of the training required to go into 'hot areas' is a three-day security training class that does not take into account intelligence monitoring and analysis. China's solicitations for the provision of security services by private companies differ considerably from the requests for proposal (RFP) issued by the United States during the Iraq and the Afghanistan conflicts.

At the same time, weak states that attract the BRI investments in the form of Chinese technology and infrastructure, more often than not, do not have the capacity to assure adequate local security. Therefore, Chinese infrastructure and personnel become easy prey to politically motivated rebel groups, or even criminal gangs. Most of the SOEs and the private Chinese firms involved in the BRI are not yet cognizant of the full spectrum of threats they are likely to face.

The method and information required to produce the type of risk assessment required for contemporary Chinese SOE operations abroad include the following.

First and foremost there is the need to understand the impact of a project in the region where the SOE will operate. This assessment is a critical part of the overall country risk scenario. Most of the time, disease, local disputes and car crashes generate more victims than the average terrorist attack. The root of the problem is not only related to the lack of security and risk managers inside the SOEs but also to the different risk perceptions that Chinese companies have compared to their Western counterparts. The political risk and the possible social media fallout that a kidnapped or killed Chinese citizen can generate back home are finally increasing the level of awareness. At the same time, a deeper understanding of the specific potential risks with Chinese characteristics could enable special insurance companies and security providers to address the SOEs actual requirements.

The first characteristic related to Chinese ODI is that most of the time it involves a greater scale compared to the other projects run in the host country. Chinese SOEs are prone to move swiftly from one project to next, engaging in a steep learning curve each time as they attempt to adapt to local necessities and habits. At the same time, sole reliance on Chinese workers who are segregated in gated compounds near to worksite produces anti-Chinese sentiment due to the perception of the perceived loss of local jobs and the suspicion that environmental degradation is taking place inside the compound. Typically, the small segment of the local community that provides goods and service to the Chinese companies increases the bitterness in the other part of the community that is cut out from the sudden influx of Yuan.

Chinese management, which is duly focused on project delivery while preparing to jump into the next financing opportunity, fails to read the local community before and during the project implementation. The managers typically rely heavily on the illusion that the central government of the host country will preserve their safety and intervene to protect their businesses. Therefore, creating winner and losers in a local community promotes the growth of anti-Chinese sentiments. As a result of being perceived just as 'a resource consuming exercise', risk mapping of local communities' stakeholders is a necessary, unavoidable task.

While Beijing has already acknowledged these risks, the problem is too often simplistically characterized as just another terrorist threat. Undoubtedly terrorism is increasingly in the news, but more disruptive threats to the Chinese investments are tied to the tensions that a project creates as well as the local criminal efforts to exploit the Chinese SOEs weaknesses.

While the employment of the growing number of private Chinese PSCs could increase the BRI's security footprint, there are still a lot of regulatory grey areas to confront. The Chinese PSCs require a proper screening and a certification process to enable them bid on security service provision. At the same time, a solid code of conduct with meaningful enforcement by the Chinese central government needs to be in place before Chinese PSCs are allowed to operate abroad. Screening for core competencies is the first step that Beijing needs to implement.

The second step is related to the analysis of a possible conflict of interest between the SOEs and the service provider. In this respect, there is still an open debate on which branch of the government should be in charge of the screening process. Several ministries from Foreign Affairs to Public Security have claimed jurisdiction over the oversight of private sector PSCs. In strict legal terms, there is still the need to define the responsibilities that the SOEs will have in case of brutality or another kind of damage that the PSC could enact on their behalf.

Another mid- to long-term problem is related to the need for transparency, not only during the provision of security services but also in the financial transactions between SOEs, PSCs and different subcontractors. Without a clear set of rules and regulations that are both practical and enforceable, it will be almost impossible to trace asset transfers and funding.

Multiple financial transactions across the globe originating from the SOEs headquarters as well as from the regional units in a broad network of banking institutions could be prone to abuse. To avoid corruption, illegal transactions or even money laundering schemes, PSC funding has to abide by a strict control on banking transfer regulations that promote transparency and accountability. Nevertheless the economic value of the Chinese PSC market is still difficult to quantify due to SOEs byzantine accounting regulations. An estimate from the Chinese Security Association quantifies the overseas yearly security expenses for the gas and oil sector by the 'three sisters': China National Petroleum Corporation, Sinopec Group and China National Offshore Oil Corporation around US$2 billion.

For each project, specific local conditions and necessities have to be taken into account, starting with the evaluation of the effectiveness in the employment of foreign forces, local ones or a mix of the two. Sometimes the exclusive use of foreign contractors could provide excellent results that eliminate the insider threat of radicalized local elements. In other cases, the use of foreign security personnel could ignite a process of radicalization that could have been dormant without the influx of external pressure.

Regarding human resource management, Chinese security sectors are still promoting a culture of a 'race to the bottom' in order to cut costs and improve profitability relying on competition that focusing on the lowest price. A business culture of high-level service provision must be substituted for the current approach that tends to favour the lower bidder. The role of training and nurturing of qualified and well-paid security officials must replace human resource procedures that up to now have failed miserably to attract talent.

The Chinese central government, which is the driving force to develop China PSC efficiency and accountability, is in the process of promoting changes not only in the overseas deployment but also in the local security arena. While the private security sector in Mainland China has still a limited range of functions, it is not difficult to foresee the development of auxiliary police services, following the example of the Singaporean auxiliary police. In this case, transparency and a reliable legal framework are the cornerstones for a long-term efficient, effective and economical provision of security services. Present dangers to the Chinese workers and infrastructures have demonstrated to Beijing that just 'throwing money at the problem' is not always the most viable solution.

The expansion of Chinese ODI along the BRI has amplified the magnitude of a possible international crisis that China may face in the near future. Consequently, the threats to China's enterprises and Chinese workers based on foreign soil are expected to increase. An efficient cooperation model among the relevant Chinese governmental agencies, including the SOEs and the private security sector is a feasible solution to sustain a BRI win-win outcome. The opportunity, if addressed with the appropriate measures, will successfully mitigate the risks to the BRI.

The danger is that failure to understand, prevent and mitigate these risks in a timely manner will jeopardize not only the entire BRI but also China's promise of sustainable development.

1.2 Securing the Belt and Road Initiative

> The value of any PowerPoint briefing on China is inversely proportional to the number of Sun Zi quotes in the briefing. (Mulvenon's Third Law)

The market for force with Chinese characteristics is influencing demand and offer for private security services. The shift in PSC requirements from the West to the East has already started. The 2016 attacks on Chinese personnel and infrastructures unambiguously illustrated the gravitas of risk confronting Chinese companies. The BRI's requirements for the provision of security services by private companies are quite different from the US engagement in large-scale conflicts. 'China's private army' is a key pillar in sustaining the expansion of Chinese outbound investments but the overall sector is in dire need of proper regulations, efficiency and professionalism.

During a routine day of work at the Chinese Embassy in Kyrgyzstan, Chinese officials were taken by surprise by the explosion wave that hit the Chinese diplomatic compound in the capital city of Bishkek. Though it is a preferred route for drugs and weapons smuggling due to the proximity with Afghanistan, the former Soviet Union republic has never shown signs for direct terrorist threats to China. On the afternoon of 31 August 2016, a suicide bomber tried to wreak havoc in the Chinese embassy. The detonation of the car bomb killed the assailant and injured three local staff members. In addition to the spread of insecurity that has characterized the young republic since its independence in 1991 and a growing concern about local Al-Qaida and Islamic State (IS) cells, this attack represented the first open threat against China in the region.

The BRI launched by President Xi Jinping in 2013, which is intended to promote economic development and exchanges between China and more than 60 countries, is gaining momentum. The BRI is not immune, however, to a number of important risks that in many instances are new to Chinese companies operating abroad.

Chinese companies, including SOEs participating in the BRI initiative (previously labelled One Belt One Road, OBOR),[1] must deal with a new set of risks to which any company operating overseas must face.

In September 2013, Chinese president Xi Jinping, during his first tour of the Central Asian republics, announced China's intention of pursuing a policy of large-scale investment, emphasized the revival of the economic and cultural ties that characterized Central Asian-China relations during the past glory of the Silk Road and promoted the rebirth of the Silk Road Economic Belt. While this date officially marked the beginning of the new Silk Road policy and rediscovery of China's continental role, the Chinese pivot to the West has its root in the Xinjiang Uyghur Autonomous Region's development policies. These policies, enacted during the mandate of Jiang Zemin and Hu Jintao, are the cornerstone of the BRI that provided a steady launch pad for Xi's vision. Moreover, the Chinese pivot to the West could also be perceived as the internationalization process of the previous 'Great Development Program of Western China'[2] launched in order to develop the country's western border in the same successful pattern that characterized the eastern provinces.

The Chinese 'renaissance' of the Silk Road is based on free transit of goods, removal of trade barriers, logistics and energy infrastructural modernization.

Just one year after his Central Asian tour in March 2014, Xi inaugurated the European tour by visiting the inland logistic port of Duisburg with undivided attention to the *Yuxinou* train that connects (three times a week) the Chongqing logistic hub with its German counterpart. The railway connection of the BRI provides Chinese goods faster access to the European Union (EU) market. At the same time, rail freight delivers EU high-tech components to the Chinese factories in less than three weeks, compared to an average of five weeks by container ship.

In 2015, the National Development and Reform Commission (NDRC), together with the Chinese Ministry of Foreign Affairs (MFA) and the Ministry of Commerce (MOFCOM), released an updated blueprint (Shaohui 2015) for the 'vision and actions on jointly building Silk Road economic belt and twenty-first century maritime Silk Road'. The blueprint presented the official line that SOEs and public officials have to follow until the release of the next five-year economic development plan (2016–2020). China's gradual rediscovery of its continental role is well documented in the blueprint that summarizes the key points of the BRI:

> The Belt and Road Initiative is a way for win-win cooperation that promotes common development and prosperity and a road towards peace and friendship by enhancing mutual understanding and trust, and strengthening all-round exchanges. The Chinese government advocates peace and cooperation, openness and inclusiveness, mutual learning and mutual benefit. It promotes practical cooperation in all fields, and works to build a community of shared interests, destiny and responsibility featuring mutual political trust, economic integration and cultural inclusiveness.

The transformative appeal of China's BRI is also related to good governance and institution building across Eurasia. From the EU side, several heads of state officially pledged their support for the BRI aiming to attract more a growing share of the Chinese ODI. Even so, however, there is still no common EU guiding policy for engaging China and assessing long-term social and political effects of the new Silk Road initiative. The EU need for Chinese financial support to develop infrastructural projects to improve local economies has not been obscured by the ongoing crisis. Also, a deeper EU involvement and participation in the BRI could defuse possible suspicions among Asian countries and United States over covert Chinese economic and political ambitions. Russia has already started to move in this direction as Putin's competing policies of the 'Iron Silk Road' and the Eurasian Economic Union (EEU) consider the BRI as an opportunity and not a threat, albeit aims to contain Chinese economic invasion.[3] Therefore, a successful implementation of these programmes, along with Russia's ability to reform its system of governance and political control, would make these two actors significant agenda setters in an inchoate new global order (Kozyrev 2015).

From the US point of view, the US Secretary of State John Kerry's Central Asian tour in November 2015 represented the first US high-level visit since the announced US disengagement from the Afghan conflict. Although President Obama had confirmed that the projected US military personnel that will remain in Afghanistan will not decrease (Raghavan et al. 2015), the US need for military bases in Central Asia has already ended. In 2014, with the termination of the Northern Distribution Network (NDN) road and rail transit route for military supplies, the closure of the US and NATO bases in Manas (Kyrgyzstan) and near Dushanbe (Tajikistan) followed shortly. With the closure of these military bases, the US foreign policy in Central Asia is no more linked to a quid pro quo stance in which the role of human rights has to be balanced with military logistics' necessities. In this regard, the US secretary of state underscored how the Central Asian republics multi-vector foreign policy needs to take into consideration the role of the United States as a counterbalance to the pressure from Chinese and Russian neighbours. Other than through media communiqués, the US proposition could not dent the Chinese economic dominance in the region nor the Russian projection of military force. Further, US policies backed by substantial economic investment could revive the former US secretary of state Hillary Clinton's policy for the revitalization of the ancient Silk Road.

Cynicism over the effort to promote regional economic integration stems from perceptions among regional elites that the US role has been mostly 'talk' rather than action, but also from the fact that the United States brings little tangible investment to the table yet has been a greater enthusiast of regional cooperation than the Central Asian governments themselves (Feigenbaun 2015).

After the unveiling of the BRI action plan, the gross export among China and the partner countries has increased by 26%, reaching a total value of US$480 billion by year end in 2015. In this respect, China's advantage in infrastructure construction is related to the availability of technical expertise and prompt financing. According to the Chinese MOFCOM statistics, the new economic and cooperation zones, which are already built along the BRI, surpass the total value of US$20 billion (EY 2015). Nevertheless, weak states that acquire Chinese technology and infrastructure or grant exploitation rights of natural resources to Chinese SOEs, more often than not, do not have the capacity to assure adequate local security arrangements. Hence, Chinese infrastructure and personnel become easy prey to politically motivated rebel groups, or even criminal gangs who perceive Chinese citizens as 'high-value' targets. While Chinese SOEs in the energy sector have already reached a degree of maturity in the adoption of high-standard security services[4]—due to its earlier experience encountered in the African continent—most other SOEs involved in the BRI are still unaware of the imminent dangers.

The gravitas of the risk confronting Chinese companies was unambiguously illustrated by the latest 2016 attacks. The proper set of solutions, however, is still under debate in Beijing or not even discussed among several SOEs involved in the BRI infrastructural projects. The opportunity is that if addressed with the appropriate measures, these risks can be successfully mitigated. The danger is that failure to address these risks in a timely manner will jeopardize not only the entire BRI, but also China's economic interests and initiatives elsewhere.

The problem has not gone unnoticed in Beijing. Over the last five years, the PLA's Navy (PLAN) has already showcased a mature crisis management capability in the evacuation of Chinese nationals from overseas hotspots, such as in Libya (in 2011) and, more recently, in Yemen. In the latter crisis, a joint effort between Chinese diplomatic missions in the region and PLAN warships operating in the Gulf of Aden managed to secure hundreds of Chinese nationals before transferring them from Yemen to Djibouti. This kind of operation, due to the financial and political burdens that the government has to sustain, is not often a viable solution. Therefore, the employment of small-scale privatized forces seems to provide immediate benefits in terms of efficiency, effectiveness and economy. A few years later, the People's Public Security University in Beijing started to take in to serious consideration the adoption of international expertise in counter-terrorism in order to train officials. Also private security training facilities have flourished in the major Chinese cities from Beijing to Shenzhen, with the support of British, Israeli, South African and Dutch experts. Since 2010, several Chinese security firms have evolved their business model from a local security provider—the so-called bodyguards for wealthy clients—to international operations with liaison offices in Beijing. Currently, the rising number of Chinese PSCs reflects the demand surge in the market for force. At the same time, the lack of a leading local corporation well underlines the novelty of the phenomenon.

While non-traditional security threats characterize only a part of the BRI, several other crises may arise in a number of countries with substantial Chinese investments. These would include social confrontations between indigenous and Chinese workers, environmental degradation issues as well as disputes over an apparent lack of corporate social responsibilities on the part of Chinese firms. Although sea transport is considered to be the main form of freight in the near future, the revival of land connectivity promoted by China via the 12,000 km rail network to the EU is going to increase in scope and size for several political, economic and security reasons (Arduino 2014). Along the maritime Silk Road the list of flashpoints is also broad and includes piracy near the Somali coast and the Malacca strait.

Therefore, several factors, if not addressed in time, could compromise the BRI long-term strategy. The exogenous factors encompass the regional socio-economic integration among the Central Asian states, the stabilization of the Afghanistan conundrum and the increasing economic competition for natural resources. At the same time, endogenous factors include the stabilization of the Xinjiang Uyghur Autonomous Region, which is a key pillar in the BRI. First and foremost among these risks is the fact that threats to Chinese enterprises and Chinese workers located in foreign countries are increasing. These threats include common criminal activity (robbery, extortion), kidnapping for ransom as well as terrorist attacks on personnel and infrastructure. The threat profile is complicated by the fact that the BRI encompasses a vast geographic footprint that includes both maritime and land routes. The task for Chinese companies is not to provide security services to isolated hot spots or other isolated areas of concern; instead, the requirement is to provide security throughout the BRI's area of operations. Consequently, there is an urgent need for Chinese companies that intend to participate in the BRI to undertake risk assessments and prepare relevant crisis management procedures.

The evolution of the BRI is forcing China's 'banking diplomacy' to embrace a broader political and security engagement with the countries involved with the initiative. Moreover, the western multilateral governance and cooperation mechanisms set up in the mid-twentieth century are not designed to keep pace with rapid economic and social developments. In this regard, the last two decades have witnessed significant shifts in the balance of geopolitical power.

In this respect, China is reinforcing its economic diplomacy and confidence building in operating multilateral organizations. The latest effort culminated with the creation of the Asian Infrastructure Investment Bank (AIIB), supported by 57 member states. Also during the 2015 EEU summit (Xin Hua 2015), Beijing was officially recognized by Moscow as the leading economic actor in one of the BRI's key area, the Central Asian arena. During the past ten years, Central Asia's geostrategic position and natural resource availability has attracted massive Chinese investments, causing the region to become progressively drawn into the Chinese economic sphere of influence, while Russia still maintains the monopoly over security. Furthermore the Afghan stabilization process influences the overall security nexus in this area. After the Ukrainian crisis was ignited by the annexation of Crimea, the Russian Federation has improved economic, politic and security ties with China. The employment of Russian volunteers to support the Ukrainian independents has also highlighted another market opportunity. Now the Chinese SOEs may also hire highly trained former Russian military personnel. Two Russian companies have already set up their offices in Hong Kong to promote security services focused on Mainland China. The selling pitch against the other international PSCs is quite straightforward: 'Russian contractors are employable for a fraction of the price of their western counterparts.'[5] Moreover, in the operation involving Central Asia, command of the Russian language is an additional asset.

While China's BRI land route initiative is gaining traction with new railway lines linking China to Europe via Central Asia, the number of crises that the Chinese SOEs operating in the region are going to face is proportionally increasing. Threats range from regional political and social instability, such as from the border clashes between Tajikistan and Kyrgyzstan or the Kyrgyz ethnic violence in Osh (2010) to the increasing protest and act of violence erupted between Chinese SOEs' worker and the local populations, such as the accident at Aktogay copper mine (Kazakhstan, 2015).

With regard to the Eurasian Land Bridge, Central and South Asia are going to play a predominant role in not only balancing among great powers but also forcing a steadier Chinese stance in the regional security policy. The overall Chinese strategy in the region encompasses different roles ranging from energy security maintenance, regional economic integration and hydro-resources management to counter-terrorism measures. More than a decade ago, China engaged the young Central Asian republics in a long-term strategic embrace that currently is showing its influence. This does not mean that either Russia or the United States has been fully displaced. But Beijing's strategy of developing investment projects that both sides find genuinely beneficial, and avoiding all discussions of domestic political affairs, has made it an increasingly more attractive foreign partner (Olcott 2013).

Remarkably, the year 2015 marks the 60th anniversary of bilateral diplomatic relations between China and Afghanistan. In this respect, the development of the BRI initiative encompasses Afghanistan, not only as China's neighbouring country but also as key actor in several economic projects. Not only China but also Russia and neighbouring countries are concerned that a rapid deterioration of Kabul's grip over the country's security is going to destabilize South and Central Asia, increasing the chances of Islamic extremism (Bortnikov 2015).[6] Afghan uncertainty is casting a wider shadow over the local Chinese direct investment, with particular regard to the Sino-Pakistan economic corridor, worth US$63 billion. In case of a sudden collapse of Kabul's government, the damaging ripple effects will not only affect China's larger economic footprint in Central Asia and its own western borders but it will reach the EU. However, the BRI necessitates a wide range of security considerations along both the maritime and land routes.

As already mentioned, China's requirements for the provision of security services by private companies are quite different from the services required by the United States during the Iraq and the Afghanistan conflicts. Due to the growing needs for PSCs services, the evolution of Chinese PSCs is posed to be a key feature for years to come.

During the last 15 years, the hybrid conflicts and the growth of terrorist threats across the globe have increasingly provided a fertile ground for the proliferation of a new breed of international private military security corporations. At present, the growth of the Chinese security market far exceeds the shrinking budgets of industrialized Western nations available to corporations to devote to the private security sector. Therefore, international competition between PSCs in entering the Chinese market is fierce. A common problem persists among these global private security firms, however, which derives from their hitherto 'one size fits all' approach. A key issue here is that they fail to take into account the operational culture of Chinese SOEs. Their relative inexperience in surmounting the cultural barriers inherent in their engagement with Chinese companies oftentimes leads to missed opportunities. At the same time, the learning curve imposed on the Chinese PSCs can be very steep indeed. Moreover, mistakes deriving from unforced errors such as 'lost in translations' in this sector are not granted a second chance.

The threat of terrorist and criminal violence is not limited to the BRI. Other crises may arise in countries where Chinese companies operate. Potential friction points may be the result of social confrontations between indigenous and Chinese workers, or conflicts sparked by an overall lack of corporate social responsibilities, such as environmental degradation. Therefore, the evolution of Chinese PSCs towards an efficient model that could provide security assessments, scenario planning, crisis prevention and mitigation is one of the key elements required to contribute to long-term international economic cooperation and sustainable development that is at the core of the BRI. The deadly terrorist attacks that have cost the life of Chinese nationals at home and abroad have also increased the awareness for improved training and intelligence gathering by public and private forces. Since 2014 the People's Public Security University[7] in Beijing has officially developed a dedicated training course for counter-terrorist officials.

1.3 Security Privatization with Chinese Characteristics

The expansion of Chinese outbound investments, aimed to sustain the increased need for natural resources, has amplified the magnitude of a possible international crisis that China may face in the near future. Consequently, the threats to China's enterprises and Chinese workers based on foreign soil are expected to increase. Fragile states that acquire Chinese technology and infrastructure or that grant exploitation rights of natural resources to Chinese SOEs do not have the capacity to assure adequate security. Therefore, Chinese infrastructure and personnel could be an easy target by politically motivated rebel groups, or even criminal gangs who perceive Chinese citizens as wealthy targets. At the same time, China's economic diplomacy and non-intervention policy is gradually shifting towards a more assertive posture on international affairs. During the race to acquire hydrocarbons and other natural resources, China has heavily invested in several unstable areas. Additionally, the kidnapping of 29 Chinese by Sudanese rebels in 2012 well highlights a trend that Beijing has taken into serious account in the near future.

Although the rising and falling cycle of the security services privatization is nothing new, the research on Chinese PSCs is still surrounded by uncertainty. The impact of 'Private Security Companies with Chinese Characteristics' is going to profoundly affect the security landscape, and an early adoption of internationally agreed rules and regulations will foster transparency, efficiency and sustainable development.

Failing to include China in an international code of conduct could allow history to repeat itself, as it happened during the African postcolonial wars that have been negatively affected by the employment of highly trained but unaccountable mercenaries.

Compared to the United States, China is not engaged in large-scale conflicts and does not have at present a necessity to outsource logistical and infrastructural services in war zones.[8] Nevertheless, the necessity for security protection and emergency evacuation in different areas of the globe is driving Beijing to formally privatize various security roles. Numerous trouble spots from Afghanistan, Egypt, Libya, Pakistan, Iraq and Sudan contain a volatile combination of Chinese investments and clear and present dangers.

Furthermore, during the last few decades, kidnapping and ransom (K&R),[9] from South America to former Soviet Union's Republics, has become a lucrative business targeting foreign corporate CEOs and specialized foreign workers. Following China's growth as a leading world economy, it is plausible to infer an increase in kidnappings for Chinese SOEs' CEOs, as well as for wealthy Chinese tourists in different areas of the world.

As a result of the Chinese Foreign Service personnel and SOEs operating abroad, China is facing the necessity to formalize a trend that started several years ago in the oil and mining sectors, which is the employment of PSCs.

Two key points distinguish the impact of Chinese PSCs in protecting Chinese outbound investments and citizens: first, the Chinese economic power and SOEs influence over the international private security market, and, second, the necessity for the international community to engage China in a common definition of roles and boundaries in the privatization of the state monopoly of violence.

War/conflict	*Contracted personnel*	*Military*	*Ratio*
Revolution	1500 (Est)	9000	1:6 (Est)
Mexican/American	6000 (Est)	33,000	1:6 (Est)
Civil War	200,000 (Est)	1,000,000	1:5 (Est)
World War I	85,000	2,000,000	1:20
World War II	734,000	5,400,000	1:7
Korea	156,000	393,000	1:2.5
Vietnam	70,000	359,000	1:6
Persian Gulf War	5200	541,000	1:100
Rwanda/Somalia/Haiti	No records kept	N/A	N/A
Balkans	5000–20,000	(Varied) 20,000	Up to 1.5:1
Iraq	95,461	95,900	1:1
Afghanistan	112,092	79,100	1.42:1

Source: Office of the Under Secretary of Defense for Acquisition, Technology and Logistics https://www.acq.osd.mil/dpap/pacc/cc/history.html

The significance of these two variables will be relevant not only to the security arena but also to a broader area including peace building for countries that benefit from abundant natural resources but rely on fragile state structures. Engaging China's PSCs in an internationally agreed code of conduct will also enhance efficiency and oversight. At the same time, the code of conduct will enable the international community and China's ODI receivers to promote accountability and sustainable development.

Examples of Beijing's economic influence in shaping international institutions are already common, ranging from the support to ASEAN members or Central Asian countries to avoid multilateral confrontations. While it seems clear that China's growing economic might is actively influencing political outcomes, the role of Chinese SOEs as the main contractors for Chinese and the international PSCs does not seem to be linked with a hidden political agenda at this time.[10] At the same time, Western observers and reports are prone to point to the Chinese PSCs' personnel's previous links with the PLA both at the management and at field levels. The top management's previous experience in the armed forces is perceived not only as a source of business contacts but also as a forefront for the PLA and the central government cover support to the expansion of the Chinese security footprints abroad.

1.4 Chinese Approach to PSC Employment: 'Crossing the River Feeling the Stones'

Without taking into account the overseas Chinese communities, more than a million Chinese workers are employed all around the globe and the Chinese MFA is in charge of the mapping of migrant workers distribution. This is a daunting task itself without taking into account that large numbers of workers operate in unpredictable zones, such as Afghan Mes Aynak copper mine by China Metallurgical Group, China National Petroleum Corporations South Sudan's oil wells, Ethiopia ITC network by Huawei-ZTE and Minmetal Nord Korea mining areas near the Chinese border.

Several Chinese PSCs emerged onto the international arena, employing a mix of local and foreign resources. The mix changes with respect to each specific requirement depend heavily on foreign expertise in risk assessment and the use of armed personnel. Chinese PSCs—with some rare exceptions related to maritime security—are barred by the MFA to employ Chinese armed contractors. Moreover, this trend strikes several resemblances with the industrial joint ventures (JVs) between Chinese and foreign corporations that have characterized the last three decades of Chinese gross domestic product (GDP) double-digit growth. Similarly, Chinese PSCs are utilizing foreign expertise and best practices in combination with their preferential access to the state-owned contractors. The main question, as has happened in several sectors of the Chinese economy—that benefitted from foreign technology transfers—is when the Chinese PSCs will feel confident enough to avoid any external help and utilize only local resources.

Therefore, it is possible to assume that the learning curve of 'Made in China' private security forces will be similar to those of Chinese JVs that employed Western technology transfers and foreign workers' best practices to achieve international standards. Discounting the time necessary to fill the gap in reaching international efficiency standards, another problem arises in the employment of Chinese PSCs. The use of 'Chinese only contractors', besides being economical compared to the use of the Western counterparts, could foster the 'Chinese fear' syndrome—as an example, in areas such as Central Asia where local populations harbour resentment towards Chinese migrant workers since the tsar times (Arduino, China in Central Asia. A new economic, security and logistic network 2015), the use of private Chinese contractors could be perceived as PLA related or at least as officially endorsed by Beijing. Therefore, the economic and political negative spillovers could overshadow in the long term the short-term financial gains.

Nevertheless, one key point is already clear: while the Chinese MFA and state insurance companies are still debating on the use of Chinese PSCs, the business opportunity for reaping high profits is already being perceived by a growing number of local and international security service providers. Also, increasing instability and a growing need for protective services by Chinese enterprises have attracted a large number of international players looking for cooperation with the emergent local PSCs.

The recent waves of Chinese PSCs could be divided in four macro groups:

1. Domestic companies focused on basic personnel close protection and credit recovery.
2. Domestic companies that have evolved from the first category, offering more specialized services ranging from IPR protection, corporate security, HR security management and logistic armoured protection.
3. Domestic companies that cooperate with foreign ones in order to provide local bidding support on Chinese tenders for international security services, risk assessment and overseas support to Chinese insurance companies.
4. Chinese companies with a developed international background in security services that cooperate with the Chinese MFA and large SOEs.

The first macro group involves thousands of companies that are benefitting from a cheap workforce, some municipal or provincial links to police and military police officials, and a favourable environment due to the lack of precise regulations in this line of business. The growing business segment is not gone unnoticed and bigger players are going to tap this market segment, an example being the electronic distributor giant Guo Mei planned to develop a training facility for professional bodyguards in Mainland China.

Also, the second macro group is evolving at a fast pace due to the increased need of IPR protection and corporate anti-espionage by Chinese brands that are becoming recognized in the international arena, not only for their cheap and low-quality 'Made in China' production but for competitive and innovative products. This group offers a more sophisticated glimpse of the market trends, with companies such as Keen Risk Solutions from Shenzhen, but is only marginally related to companies that are going to evolve in a full PSC. Global players such as Control Risks are already operating with offices in China, providing consultancy services on anti-bribery and corruption policies as well as risk assessment for Merger and Acquisition (M&A).

The third macro group encompasses a wide range of different actors that are set to leap into the fourth group of mature PSCs due to a different set of variables including a strong network of connections with big SOEs, the Ministry of Defence, the MOFA and the banking and insurance sectors. The actors in this group have started some initial contact with international PSCs in order to upgrade their knowledge base and overall international capabilities and risk assessment. Companies such as Jin Wei Security in Shanghai, in cooperation with the British NGS, provide international security services for Chinese CEOs in low-security threat areas during their business trips abroad. During the Milan Expo 2015, Jin Wei security personnel provided unarmed security to Chinese VIPs visiting the World Expo site in Italy, as well as local drivers and emergency medical evacuation. At the same time, the main constrains to their growth is not the lack of suitable clients but inner weaknesses related to the scarcity of properly trained domestic human resources, especially the ones with skill sets ranging from risk assessment, logistical expertise, and foreign cultures and languages. Also, several factors concur to constrain their international expansion—from the lack of risk management and insurance coverage to their employee, to unattractive premiums to work in hazardous areas. Foreign experts also move this critic even to the more mature Chinese actors underlining how the focus on cutting costs produces high-risk acceptance behaviour (Erickson and Collins 2012). Currently, only the main insurance companies such as Ping An are actively researching risks and managing threats. In the near future, Chinese insurance companies are going to acquire a significant share of the market for force.

The fourth group is also experiencing a growth, albeit at a slower pace, than the other three. In companies belonging to the mature side of the security market, it is possible to list some interesting actors such as the following: VSS Security Group, which is involved with the securities duties for CNOPC in Iraq and Afghanistan; Huawei Security Company,[11] which provides security services in hot areas including K&R insurance and global response services in cooperation foreign partners; Dingtai Anyuan

International Security & Defense Limited (DTAY), which operates mainly in Iraq and Afghanistan; Huaxin Security Company, which cooperates with international corporations, especially those based in Singapore on anti-piracy security, and also on behalf of COSCO shipping company, providing close protection armed guards on ships operating in dangerous transit lines; and De Wei Security, which follows the protection of Chinese oil and gas sector from Ethiopia to Iraq. Larger national PSCs such as RWY that count on 200,000 security personnel are also probing cooperation with local PSCs in Central and South Asia.

This group does not present a mature leader and is not committed—at the moment—to cooperate and share experience in order to improve the overall situation. Several international firms are already operating in China with representative offices, preferential agreements with local partners and even registered enterprises under the Chinese law such as the case of the Spanish international security firm Prosegur in Shanghai. Several other companies prefer to market their services in areas that support the role of Chinese PSCs abroad, such as the case of the Hong Kong company, which is registered in Beijing as logistic service provider, and Frontier Services Group (FSG), which benefits from the experience of the group chairman Mr Erik Prince (Prince and Coburn 2013),[12] founder of Blackwater.

According to a research published by the Chinese Think Tank Phoenix (PTT 2016) in cooperation with Qinghua University in Beijing, the ranking of the top ten Chinese security firms is as follows:

1. G4S
2. Control Risks
3. Beijing Dewei Security Service Co. Ltd.
4. Zhongguo Anbao China Security Industry Co., Ltd.
5. Huaxin Zhongan (Beijing) Security Service Co., Ltd.
6. Shanghai Zhongchenwei Security Service Group Co. Ltd.
7. Beijing Dingtai Anyuan Guard & Technology Research Institute
8. Shengzhen Zhongzhou Tewei Security Consultant Co. Ltd.
9. Beijing Guanan Security & Technology Co. Ltd.
10. Shandong Huawei Security Group Ltd. Subsidiary

The service provided by this last group comprises the protection of the workers compound during large-scale energy and infrastructure projects, the security of the Chinese shipping companies vessels and logistic hubs as well as the safety of corporate official and high-value individuals travelling abroad. The ample spectrum of services is summarized in:

- Risk assessment, providing security reports in order to allow the company business feasibility study and the government mandatory security assessment
- Risk management, monitoring the evolution of the Chinese footprint and the reaction of the local stakeholders, adapting with the daily risks and threats
- Risk mitigation, coping with ongoing crisis providing medical extraction for injured personnel and Chinese nationals evacuation in cooperation with the Chinese MOFA
- Risk transfer, supporting the insurance companies to find suitable partners to share the risk burdens
- Providing security compliance audit reports on the Chinese company overseas offices
- Training security personnel and company officials

Whereas the PLA local involvement in the Chinese business environment has been tamed in the last decade, the role of SOEs in shaping foreign policies has been increasing. Specifically with the use of private security firms, this trend is going to develop into more elaborate structures. With the latest purge of corrupted officials in the PLA, President Xi Jinping has accomplished a long-standing reform to detach the PLA from the entrepreneurial side of the Chinese development. In 1929, during Gutian Congress, Mao Zedong affirmed vehemently the dominance of the party over the military. Following Mao dictate that 'the Party commands the gun, and the gun must never be allowed to command the Party',[13] Xi, who is also the chairman of the Central Military Commission (CMC), started to structurally reform the PLA from the inside. In order to correlate his actions with Mao's legacy, Xi announced the reform goals during a party meeting held in the Fujian provincial city of Gutian. Since the start of the anti-corruption campaign aimed to fight 'tigers' and 'flies', high- and low-ranking officials have been sacked. Also, the PLA officials have not been spared by the anti-corruption purge, which culminated in 2014 and 2015 with the arrest of two prominent members of the CMC, General Xu Caihou and General Guo Boxiong, respectively. While several western China watchers (The Economist 2015) have labelled the anti-corruption campaign as a move to strengthen the personal power of

Xi, it is undoubted that downsizing and reorganization into a leaner and flexible military organization is going to benefit the PLA. Therefore, a modern and operational military apparatus that is outmost loyal to the party is going to support China's claims as a major power (Grossman and Case 2016).

At the same time, the so-called move to privatization has been steered towards more efficient public sectors where the SOEs still benefit from government support and a favourable line of credit from the state banks. Therefore, with a declining economic power held by PLA, and a growing but still not mature military industrial complex (MIC), the power distribution towards the leading SOEs is going to increase the opportunities for a large area of intervention in the shaping of international policies without the direct influence of the military.

Currently the private sector security standards are set by a group of Western companies, but with the evolution of the market's demands and conditions, it is possible to assume that mature Chinese companies will be able to attract qualified personnel and nurture their own Chinese talents. These companies will have to establish clear operational security parameters starting with the provision of medical assistance and emergency evacuation capabilities, and long-term strategy versus short-term problem-solving. An approved Chinese association with a standardized certification would be helpful to improve the market and operational conditions, also taking in to account all the variables ranging from investments in dangerous environments to business leaders' travel risk. In the meantime, the PSC that aspires to become the leading security provider has to take into serious consideration the organization capacity to absorb new competencies, which have taken international PSCs decades, and costly errors, to develop. Therefore, adaptability and organization learning is one of the key pillars for the new Chinese PSCs. *Mutatis mutandis* from the Chinese industrial sector it is possible to infer that as soon as a leading PSC will be recognized among its peers, fierce talent poaching will start. Chinese managers currently operating in the PSC field with a good command of foreign languages and some international exposure are a scarce resource, and have on average hold less than five years' experience in the field. Implementing new changes while growing exponentially on a global scale will be an imposing challenge, and in the security field, the process of trial and errors can be very costly in terms of a negative spillover that a mishandled crisis situation will generate. Also, some Chinese PSCs underline[14] how foreign operators, mainly British, have better experience in communicating with local populations not only in terms of risk assessments and intelligence gathering but also in dealing with daily workforce issues. In different areas ranging from Africa to Central Asia and the Far East, several of the threats to the Chinese enterprises profitability came from the inside, and are mainly related to the problems between the local and Chinese workforces.

Focusing on overtime and productivity bonuses, Chinese workers often spend a year abroad returning home only during the Chinese New Year, as their main objective is to capitalize as much as possible on their only source of income, long working hours. At the same time local workforces that are used to different employment conditions perceive the Chinese worker as a threat to their lifestyle, and possibly damaging to their surrounding environment. Often small strikes for better pay lead to mass gatherings and violent revolts towards Chinese infrastructure and personnel (BBC 2012).

At the same time the new role of PSCs could also foster innovation and adaptation of new technologies in the field. Drone recognizance capabilities, matched with satellite data gathering provided by specialized PSCs, could not only foster SOEs risk assessments and strategy building but also provide affordable specialized services to other PSCs that do not have the need to train and maintain dedicated hardware and personnel. Additionally, Chinese PSCs providing this kind of specialized support do not need to overcome the language and cultural barriers where 'a lost in translation' could compromise an entire operation.

In the near future, PSCs with 'Chinese characteristics' are going to be a subject of increasing academic interest not only in the field directly related to the privatization of the monopoly of violence but in many more intertwined areas, ranging from international law to defence economics and peace building. The augmented role that is going to be played by the Chinese PSCs in the security arena is going to affect not only the security actors but also the security stage as a whole. The outcome is greater than the singular consequences just added together. Nevertheless the new PSC breed is going to retain some of the former advantages of the previous market-oriented security corporations, ranging from increased efficiency and cost-effectiveness to a superior flexibility towards complex and fast-changing environments. Although some of the previous advantages, such as public deniability in the use of force in international context, will be affected by the peculiar nature of Chinese enterprises. An 'all Chinese' operators team is going to be perceived by locals as Chinese government related. Perhaps physical distinguishing traits are going to be taken more in to consideration than proven links with Beijing's international agenda.

Although the rising and falling cycle of the security services privatization is nothing new, a high degree of uncertainty still surrounds the research on Chinese PSCs, uncertainty that is not due to a well-conceived shrouding of PSC activities but mostly by the emergent nature of this trend in China. The basic lack of communication and coordination among local actors is further proof. While the time frame for a mature market for local PSCs is still undefined, the need to engage China in developing commonly agreed international rules is a present necessity. Moreover, the adoption of a code of conduct is poised to benefit not only Chinese emergent capabilities but also the situation in the developing countries that receive Chinese ODI.

A mature Chinese PSC, understanding the security environment complexity, will be able to detect and counter threats posed by non-state armed actors, as well as avoid and manage crisis generated by SOE investment negative spillovers.

Therefore, it is imperative to involve China, at an early stage, in an international effort to promote transparency and accountability. Furthermore, a new breed of Chinese PSC has to provide services that benefit not only the client but also the international community, fostering the development of weak state's structures without superseding the state institutions in the monopoly of violence.

Notes

1. The Silk Road Economic Belt, together with the twenty-first-century Maritime Silk Road, commonly known as the 'One Belt and One Road' (OBOR,一带一路, *yidai yilu*) initiative. The One Belt refers to the maritime dimension and the One Road refers to the overland historical Silk Road that connected China with the West via Central Asia.
2. Zhongguo Xibu kaifa, http://www.chinawest.gov.cn/web/index.asp
3. 'Joint Statement of the Russian Federation and the People's Republic of China on the New Stage of the Comprehensive Strategic Partnership of Cooperation', Kremlin Web Site, May 20, 2014, http://kremlin.ru/supplement/1642
4. Author's interview with international security consultants involved in the oil and gas companies' protection. Beijing November 2014.
5. Author's interview with Chinese academicians specialized in security and international relations. Shanghai, June 2016.

6. Aleksandr Bortnikov, director of Russia's Federal Security Service (FSB) on the increase of IS threat to Central Asia and Commonwealth of Independent States (CIS): 'serious concerns over the escalation of tension in Afghanistan … under the banner of Islamic State…' 'FSB: Moving Part of the Taliban to DZ Resulted in Increased Threats to their Invasion of Central Asia,' *TASS*, Oct 28, 2015, http://tass.ru/politika/2384331
7. 'We urgently need to train counterterrorism specialists to improve our preventive and terror-fighting capabilities to cope with serious terrorist incidents,' said Mei Jianming, director of the Counterterrorism Research Center at the university, which is the first in China to train such professionals.' in Zhang Wei 'Chinese public security university trains anti-terror specialists.' *China Daily*, Mar 25, 2016, http://en.ce.cn/main/latest/201603/25/t20160325_9802767.shtml
8. US Central Command reported in January 2015 that 54,700 private contractors worked for the Defense Department in its areas of responsibility. http://www.acq.osd.mil/log/PS/reports/CENTCOM%20Census%20Reports/5A_January2015.pdf
9. 'K&R … a market worth about $250 m in 2006 doubled in size by 2011…' from The Economist; Schumpeter Business and Management 'Kidnap and Ransom Insurance. I'm a client … get me out of here.' Jun. 27th (2013) http://www.economist.com/blogs/schumpeter/2013/06/kidnap-and-ransom-insurance?fsrc=rss
10. Author's interviews with international PSCs operators in China. Beijing, Shanghai. June 2016.
11. 'Huawei provides internal services, but in October 2010, opened an "Overseas Service Center" in Beijing. The company's statement on the centre's opening explicitly cites the withdrawal of U.S. troops from Iraq, and the potential for a security vacuum to result, as key drivers of its decision to target the Iraq market.' Erickson and Collins 2012.
12. 'Critics may have questioned my company's tactics, but to this day no one has ever doubted our results. In some fifty thousand completed personal security detail mission, we never suffered a single loss of life or serious injury to those in our care.' Prince and Coburn 2013.
13. Mao Zedong 'Problems of War and Strategy' Sixth Plenary Session of the Sixth Central Committee of the Party November 6, (1938).
14. Interview with Beijing PSC managers that operate in Iraq protecting Chinese oil companies infrastructures. February 2015.

References

Arduino, Alessandro. 2014. *The New Silk Road*. ECRAN, Short Term Policy Brief No. 9, May. http://eeas.europa.eu/china/docs/division_ecran/ecran_is114_paper_91_the_new_silk_road_alessandro_arduino_en.pdf. Accessed 2015.

———. 2015. China in Central Asia. A New Economic, Security and Logistic Network. In *China's Power and Asian Security*, ed. Mingjiang Li and Kalyan M. Kemburi, 216. New York: Routledge.

BBC. 2012. Zambian Miners Kill Chinese Manager During Pay Protest. *BBC*, August 15. http://www.bbc.com/news/world-africa-19135435. Accessed 2015.

Bortnikov, Aleksandr. 2015. FSB: Moving Part of the Taliban to DZ Resulted in Increased Threats to Their Invasion of Central Asia. *TASS*, October 28. http://tass.ru/politika/238433. Accessed 2016.

Erickson, Andrew, and Gabe Collins. 2012. Enter China Security Firms. *The Diplomat*, February. http://thediplomat.com/2012/02/enter-chinas-security-firms/. Accessed 2015.

EY. 2015. Navigate the Belt and Road. Financial Sector Paves the Way to for Infrastructure. *EY*, August. http://www.ey.com/Publication/vwLUAssets/EY-navigating-the-belt-and-road-en/$FILE/EY-navigating-the-belt-and-road-en.pdf. Accessed 2016.

Feigenbaun, Evan A. 2015. Secretary Kerry's Visit to Central Asia. *Carnegie Endowment for International Peace*, November 1. http://carnegieendowment.org/2015/11/01/us-central-asia-secretary-kerry-s-visit/ikvj. Accessed 2016.

Grossman, Derek, and Michael Case. 2016. Xi's Purge of the Military Prepares the Chinese Army for Confrontation. *RAND*, April. http://www.rand.org/blog/2016/04/xis-purge-of-the-military-prepares-the-chinese-army.html. Accessed 2016.

Kozyrev, Vitaly. 2015. China and Russia Multiply Efforts in Global Agenda-Setting. *Jamestown Foundation*, October 2. http://www.jamestown.org/programs/chinabrief/single/?tx_ttnews%5Btt_news%5D=44450&tx_ttnews%5BbackPid%5D=789&no_cache=1#.Vl_VIp0Z6Hs. Accessed 2016.

Olcott, Martha Brill. 2013. China Unmatched Influence in Central Asia. *Carnegie Endowment for International Peace*, September 18. http://carnegieendowment.org/2013/09/18/china-s-unmatched-influence-in-central-asia-pub-53035. Accessed 2016.

Prince, Erik, and David Coburn. 2013. *Civilian Warriors: The inside Story of Blackwater and the Unsung Heroes of the War on Terror*. London: Penguin.

PTT. 2016. Haiwai anquan guangli baogao. *Phoenix*. http://pit.ifeng.com/event/special/haiwaianquanguanlibaogao/

Raghavan, Sudarsan, Sayed Salahuddin, and Mohammad Sharif Obama. 2015. Obama Outlines Plan to Keep 5,500 Troops in Afghanistan. *Washington Post*, October 15. https://www.washingtonpost.com/world/national-security/obama-expected-to-announce-new-plan-to-keep-5500-troops-in-afghanistan/2015/10/14/d98f06fa-71d3-11e5-8d93-0af317ed58c9_story.html. Accessed 2016.

Shaohui, Tian. 2015. Vision and Actions on Jointly Building Silk Road Economic Belt and 21st Century Maritime Silk Road. *Xinhua Net*, March. http://news.xinhuanet.com/english/china/2015-03/28/c_134105858.htm. Accessed 2017.

The Economist. 2015. Xi Jinping's Fight Against Corruption in the Military Continues. *The Economist*, July 31. http://www.economist.com/news/china/21660257-china-nets-its-most-senior-army-general-yet-xi-jinpings-fight-against-corruption-military. Accessed 2015.

Xin Hua. 2015. The China-proposed Silk Road Economic Belt Initiative Is Not a Competitor, But a Partnership Project for Russia: Russian PM. *Xinhua News Agency*, August 22. http://news.xinhuanet.com/english/2015-08/22/c_134544640.htm. Accessed 2015.

CHAPTER 2

From Shadow to Hype

Abstract The Belt and Road Initiative (BRI) evolving roadmap is filled by flashpoints. As China is becoming the leading world economy there is an increasing call for active participation in stabilization process and security involvement. Free riding from the US security umbrella is over. One answer is the involvement of private security providers. Since the 1990s the re-emergence of private security companies (PSCs) and the private security and military industry has been facilitated by the restructuring of the peace dividends brought by the end of the Cold War. One of the several problems related to PSCs began with the lack of an unambiguous and mutually agreed definition of what a private security firm really is. The Chinese Mainland private security market is starting now to move from an informal and fragmented setting to a more mature sector.

Keywords Market for force • PMSC • PSC • Chinese PSC • BRI security

2.1 Private Military and Security Companies: From Shadow to Hype

The curate, having turned the corner, directed, as was his wont, a look toward the little chapel, and there beheld what he little expected, and would not have desired to see. At the confluence, if we may so call it, of the two

© The Author(s) 2018

A. Arduino, *China's Private Army*,
https://doi.org/10.1007/978-981-10-7215-4_2

> narrow lanes, there were two men: one of them sitting astride the low wall; his companion leaning against it, with his arms folded on his breast. The dress, the bearing, and what the curate could distinguish of the countenance of these men, left no doubt as to their profession. They wore upon their heads a green network, which, falling on the left shoulder, ended in a large tassel, from under which appeared upon the forehead an enormous lock of hair. Their mustachios were long, and curled at the extremities; the margin of their doublets confined by a belt of polished leather, from which were suspended, by hooks, two pistols; a little powder-horn hung like a locket on the breast; on the right-hand side of the wide and ample breeches was a pocket, out of which projected the handle of a knife, and on the other side they bore a long sword, of which the great hollow hilt was formed of bright plates of brass, combined into a cypher: by these characteristics they were, at a glance, recognised as individuals of the class of bravoes. Alessandro Manzoni (The Betrothed Cap. I)

The kidnapping and killing of Chinese workers in Pakistan in 2017 and in Afghanistan in 2004, the evacuation of 35,000 Chinese workers during the collapse of Gadhafi regime in Libya, the murder of 13 Chinese sailors in the Golden Triangle area of the Mekong River, the beheading of a Chinese national by IS in Iraq and the killing of three state-owned enterprises (SOEs) corporate officials during the Bamako terrorist attack are forcing China towards an interventionist path. The Belt and Road Initiative (BRI) evolving roadmap is filled by flashpoints. As China is becoming the leading world economy there is an increasing call for active participation in stabilization process and security involvement. Free riding from the US security umbrella is over. One answer is the involvement of private security providers. Nevertheless, the private security companies (PSCs) role is still portrayed by the media as 'guns for hire' and the negative perception of private security contractors as mercenaries is still diffused. Mercenaries' historical legacy, both in the West and the East, provoked popular disdain in the profession of lance for hire. In China, the recent warlord era has left a profound mistrust over the entire concept of private soldiering.

One of the several problems related to PSCs began with the lack of an unambiguous and mutually agreed definition of what a private security firm really is (Singer 2003). Unclear boundaries associate mercenaries with PSCs, private military companies (PMCs) or global corporations that provide hybrid services ranging from logistic support, intelligence gathering, special forces training, emergency evacuation, anti-piracy protection, fixed emplacements security as well as tactical support involving the pre-emptive use of force. The term 'PSC' used in this book encompasses PMCs and global corporations that offer a mix of security services, private military security companies (PMSCs), but a clear definition of each one of the actors involved is still urgently needed. Numerous researchers address the differentiation between PSC and PMC focusing solely on the degree of force employed. Several others analyse the state's monopoly of violence privatization exclusively under culturally situated moral lenses. Both perspectives are needed, together with a broader range of disciplines, ranging from the international relations to the economic one. The lack of an unambiguous and mutually agreed definition on the private security firms' use of force deters any chance to regulate the market.

One of the latest efforts in addressing the problem is the International Code of Conduct Association (ICoCA),[1] which even includes a Chinese version[2] with its own particular set of guidelines and three Chinese registered members since 2013.[3] The ICoC was adopted on 9 November 2010 and is based on the 'Montreux Document on pertinent legal obligations and good practices for States related to operations of private military and security companies during armed conflict'. The aim of the ICoC is to raise standards globally across the PSC sector, in order to ensure that the actions of private security providers do not contravene the norms of human rights or international humanitarian law and have a positive impact on the enjoyment of human rights by individuals affected by their work.

The ICoCA is governed by a tripartite board of governments, member companies and civil society, and its membership, which currently includes 92 PSCs from 30 countries, 7 governments and 18 civil society organizations.[4] The ICoCA ensures effective implementation of the ICoC through three key processes: certifying that companies have systems and policies in place consistent with the ICoC, in-field and desk-based reviewing of member company implementation of Code commitments and facilitating access to effective remedy for individuals harmed by actions of member companies that are inconsistent with ICoC commitments. Still, the enforcement of the ICoC remains a daunting task.

A straightforward, albeit limited, definition is found in the US National Defense Authorization Act for fiscal year 2008 that describes the private security functions as the guarding of personnel, facilities or properties and any other activity with armed personnel (GSA 2008). Also, the international guidelines in the provisions and prohibitions of security services are expressed in the International Convention Against the Recruitment,

Use, Financing and Training of Mercenaries (UNTS, art. 1, December 4, 1989), but there is not a straightforward link to the national laws that have to deal with the problem. The lack of an internationally recognized and adopted framework of law and related enforcing agency lets the nation states alone in engaging the private security sector. In this respect, the PSCs benefit from a flexible global environment that permits to choose in which state one company might place the financial core interests and in which state it is possible provide lawfully security services. An example of superficiality in addressing the issue of financial paradise while forgetting the rule of law regarding the provision of mercenary recruitment and deployment is represented by the Russian PSC Moran, which used a Hong Kong shell company linked to a British Virgin Islands (BVI) one. While the BVI are well known for offering fiscal privileges avoiding tax burdens and a limited degree against financial disclosure, they being part of the British Commonwealth follow the British law in which the direct provision of private military services is strictly forbidden.

In his pioneering work, P.W. Singer defines private military firms (PMFs) as 'private business entities that deliver to consumers a wide spectrum of military and security services, once generally assumed to be exclusively inside the public context'. In 'The Market for Force: The Consequences of Privatizing Security', Deborah Avant (Avant 2005) categorizes PMSCs by the provision of external or internal security services. This latter classification well suits the Chinese case in which there is clear boundary in which PSC with augmented capabilities are to be deployed only overseas, while the evolution of local PSC is meant only as limited support to the police. In this respect it is helpful to remember how Beijing devotes almost the same amount of gross domestic product (GDP)[5] to the internal security and order maintenance as the budget devoted to the defence. Another stimulating attempt to define the role of the PMSC is to be found in Sean McFate's book *The Modern Mercenary: Private Armies and What They Mean for World Order*, which conjugates the theoretical approach with the author's personal experience in the field. Another attempt to define the sector, like 'The Markets for Force Privatisation of Security Across World Regions' (Molly Dunigan 2015), cross-references the markets for private military and security contractors in 12 nations; in this case, the analysis on China is mostly related to the internal role of PSCs as static guards or close protection. Focusing on the Chinese market for force specificities, the article by Andrew Ericson and Gabe Collins (Andrew Ericson 2012) is one of the first attempts to analyse the growing demand for Chinese PSC since the new 2010 law that regulates the sector. Moreover, Mathieu Duchatel publication (Parello-Plesner and Duchâtel 2015) *China's Strong Arm: Protecting Citizens and Assets Abroad* is a fundamental source of information on the evolution of Beijing's capabilities in addressing the emergency repatriation of Chinese nationals during international emergency crisis.

2.2 Private Security Companies Go Mainstream

The 2009 Regulation on the Administration of Security and Guarding Services,[6] enacted on 1 January 2010, defines for the first time the guidelines for the PSC market in Mainland China with some procedures for the provision of outbound security services. The new law generated a flood in security companies' registration but the typology of personnel and modus operandi did not change substantially from the past. Former links with police and military are still one of the main characteristics that almost all Chinese PSCs share. Most of PSC CEOs have previous working experiences in the state security apparatus, and managers with a former, long-standing business background are still scarce. One of the main reasons of this trend is to be found in the legal limbo that the Chinese PSCs experienced from 1993 to 2010. During this period only companies owned by the Chinese state's Public Security Bureau were permitted to register and operate PSCs. To complicate the matter, in provincial and municipal areas, far from the central government control, a more relaxed approach to the 2010 law still permits to register security companies with substandard capabilities or even under a different business scope in order to circumvent controls and operational requirements.

Mainly, these substandard companies try to avoid paying the registered capitals of Yuan 1 million, opting instead for a consulting business licence in the order of few thousand Yuan registered capitals, and also avoiding the other requirement imposed by the security law[7] with special regards to the ban in debt-collecting activities.[8] While this trend is gradually changing for good, the numbers of bodyguards and credit recovery agents operating in a grey area are still in the hundreds of thousands. A more strict approach is related to the permit to carry weapons and is regulated by an older law promulgated in 2002 referring to the Administration of Use of Guns by Full-time Guards and Escorts.[9]

The Chinese trend in the privatization of the monopoly of security is not as fast as the case of the US private support to the military effort, but it is still experiencing a shift from the state monopoly to the privatization of some police functions such as traffic assistant, fixed guard emplacement or security support during public events that require crowd management. In this respect the major share of the privatization trend is related to PSCs operating outside the country boundaries in support of the Chinese overseas interest. Unfortunately in this case the Regulation on the Administration of Security and Guarding Services does not provide clear and straightforward operating procedures, as it was drafted with a close look to the national security market. The law specifically entitles sole responsibility to the Public Security Department of the State Council for supervising and administering security and guarding services throughout the country, declining the public security organs at local levels these responsibilities under their jurisdiction. At the same time, the paternity over the PSCs' international monitoring is mutually claimed by the State Council, the Ministry of Foreign Affairs (MFA), the Chinese Supreme Court in terms of corporate liabilities and even the military. Another problem deriving by the new law is related to the criminal liabilities that the PSC CEOs have in respect of the state secret. The SOEs' internal information, even the ones related to insignificant business plan, could constitute a state secret, as the SOEs are a part of the state apparatus. The application of the sanction regarding the divulgement of a state secret could lead to life imprisonment and are not to be easily dissed as a formality by international PSCs cooperating with a local counterpart. At the moment there are no known cases of state secret infringement in the cooperation between national and international PSCs due to the novelty of the business model, but there are plenty of examples drawn from far simpler business cooperation in the past. The case of the Australian mining company Rio Tinto in China showcases how the information of Chinese iron ore production divulged to the Australian counterpart has led to the detention of Rio Tinto senior executive in Shanghai for more than ten years for 'selling state secrets'.[10]

Since the late 1990s, stories about corporations providing specialized security services routinely appear in the media's mainstream narrative.

This phenomenon underlines how the market for force, or muscle as it is referred to in polite circles, is not just expanding; it is now regarded as a normal activity. During 2008 Beijing Olympics and 2010 Shanghai World Expo, local PSCs started to cooperate with foreign counterparts, forging links that are benefiting their internationalization. By 2010 in China, the media began to cover the role of locally owned Chinese PSCs in the international arena. Since 2014, newspapers and magazines such as

Global Times (Xin 2015) ('Chinese security companies in great demand as overseas investment surges' by Xie Wenting, 23 June 2016) and the *Wen Ming Daily* have commented favourably on the internationalization of the Chinese PSCs and recognized that there is a growing market for local security providers. The final blessing for the Chinese private security sector occurred when President Xi called (Xin Hua 2015) for increased efforts to ensure the safety of Chinese nationals and organization overseas after the killing of three Chinese during a terrorist attack in Bamako, Mali, in 2015. Beside Chinese journalists, Chinese academicians and party officials have also focused their interest in the role of private security providers that rely on the skill sets offered by People's Liberation Army (PLA), People's Armed Police (PAP) and the MFA.

Regrettably, the media narrative portrays only a small part of the picture that involves PSCs. The controversy is related to several concomitant factors: a vague definition of a PSC; limited financial accountability in the transaction between the PSC and the contractor; a negative bias that has characterized the use of 'mercenaries' since the Westphalia treaty (1648); the lack of an enforceable legal framework to regulate the private sector PSCs; and the stigma of 'lone wolf mercenaries' from the Africa's post-colonial conflicts, just to name a few.

Since Blackwater's[11] Nisour Square incident in Iraq,[12] the media have portrayed the role of PSCs to the general public as 'guns for hire'. The contemporary negative perception of 'mercenaries' is still linked to the despicable actions committed by private soldiers during Africa's postcolonial wars. Also, the negative public perception of PMSCs is the result of almost three centuries of transformation of post-Westphalia national armies, where the soldier-citizen under the control of a national command authority has replaced the 'lance for hire' that provided services to the highest bidder.

Since the end of the Cold War, the scope and size of services provided by PSCs have increased due to several interrelated factors, including:

- Demobilization of large armies after the collapse of the Soviet Union, which resulted in an increased availability of qualified operators in the market, ranging from special forces to intelligence and technical personnel.
- Changing dynamic of warfare towards transnational low-intensity conflicts and legitimacy of the role of non-state actors in the use of force (Gray 2009) and the recent paradigm of hybrid war.[13]

- Economic globalization, an increase in foreign direct investments and transnational natural resources exploitation have increased the requirement for PSC services among private corporations operating abroad.
- National armies' imperatives to preserve the expensive military equipment, to avoid incurring its loss.
- Cyber warfare shift from military threat to a transversal menace to the public and private sectors.

Since the 1990s the re-emergence of PSCs and the private security and military industry has been facilitated by the restructuring of the peace dividends brought by the end of the Cold War. NATO's redefinition of strategies that do not anticipate a Soviet-style invasion of Europe's western front has led to a progressive decrease of defensive budgets among European countries and a parallel downsizing of the armed forces (NATO 2016). An increased role in the security sphere by the PMSCs has progressively led to the erosion of the Western countries' monopoly over the means of force, in favour of a globalized and privatized market for the provision of force. Two conflicts in Iraq and one in Afghanistan have demonstrated the increased role of the PSCs followed by a concomitant rise of anxiety over their role.

In the twentieth century, from Africa's internal struggle, to Latin America's high violence rate and the Arab world's turbulence, the terms 'governance voids' and 'failed state' have become the norm. Nevertheless, asymmetry in conflict is not a new phenomenon. The contemporary nature of conflict itself is changing the interaction between state and non-state actors. From terrorists to irregular fighters, non-state entities are dictating the rhythm in the conflict progression. The asymmetric tools employed against state actors allow the non-state actors to direct the time, the place and the terms in which the force is used. The answer from the state is that even if it is effective, it is not proportionate and is limited by financial constraints and social norms. The power vacuum generated by weak or absent state government allows other actors to exert their own authority that promotes violence and creates instability. Moreover, the traditional international relations view of a state-centric world does not consider non-state actors as a key component (Gray 1997).

> As for armed groups, NSA's (Non-State Actors) have traditionally been considered challengers without formal responsibility, while governments are

> the upholders of order and security, the providers of public goods. Yet, it is increasingly recognised that NSA's are key actors in contemporary armed conflicts and that interest in studying them is well-based in both academia and policy research. (Smith 2006)

The new era of conflict, characterized by global security concerns and uncertainty, well represent the re-emerging role of the PSCs. New paradigms of war such as 'war amongst people'[14] are changing old scenarios based on 'total war' with a shift from industrial wars to non-industrial wars against non-state opponents.

> This endemic problem is the result of the shift in the paradigm of war and the continue resistance to it: politicians and soldiers are still thinking in terms of the old paradigm and trying to use their conventionally configured forces to that end—whilst the enemy and the battle have changed. (Smith 2006)

The cyber dimension of the future conflict and threats fostered an increased role of professionals operating outside the realm of the government security. In the last decade, several industrial sectors ranging from financial services, communications and telecommunications, manufacturing, healthcare, entertainment and media have witnessed an increase in sophisticated cyber attack that deviates from the lone hacker modus operandi to a more coordinated one from organized crime, cyber PSCs and foreign government (PWC 2016). The role of cyber PSC is even more difficult to define than the 'brick and mortar' counterpart. In this respect the virtual dimension blurs the national boundaries and the differentiation from defensive and offensive role even more. Also in the cyber dimension, the risk awareness and the threats monitoring are essential in order to prevent and contain eternal attacks. The role of in-house cyber security capabilities is of primary importance, but the costs and the comprehension related to this exercise are not viable to the small and medium companies. As in the case of PSCs providing risk monitoring and simulation, cyber PSCs' cyber security is capable of acting on analytic inputs related to evolving threats. Big data and data analytics are at the forefront of cyber security, but the cost in maintaining advanced algorithms, high-level processing power and massive data storage capabilities induce a high entry-level bar for most of the public and private corporations. In order to allocate in an efficient manner the already-scarce resources, public and private companies plan to contract the security service providers for the defence of their cyber domain. While the costs in maintaining the cyber security structures are one of the primary constraints, the scarcity of skilled data analyst and cyber security experts compounds the problem (PWC 2016). Lack of time, funds and human resource inside the company increases the need of external support by skilled cyber PSCs. This market trend is not gone unnoticed in China, and the local cyber PSCs are actively promoting their services in this market for force growing niche.

At the same time, in China one of the main concerns over the deployment of PSCs is not related to ethical or political uneasiness; instead, the trepidation is related to the SOEs' willingness to pay and the lack or inadequate understanding of risk management. A survey among several Chinese PSCs operating on behalf of SOEs outside China, albeit the small sample size admittedly does not provide any scientific proof, indicates through a high response rate that price is a major driver in the choice of a security service provider. This indicates that the decision process used to engage a PSC is dangerously imbalanced. Instead of focusing on the risk profile, SOEs that retain a PSC do so based primarily on price sensitivity. This creates vulnerabilities, for the simple reason that the penalty for such a dubious decision is paid for in risk to the SOEs' employees and assets.

After an incident has occurred and the media begin to project a bad image of the SOE in question, only then is there a realization within the SOE that a security and risk assessment and crisis management protocol should have been embedded in the corporate structure and business model from the very beginning. An increasing number of Chinese corporations are establishing special economic development zones in dangerous areas around the world, but the perception of the risks and threats to personnel and infrastructure is not given the prominence it deserves. No risk mitigation and crisis managements protocols are being established. Hence without a clear understanding by the SOE's CEO and CSO of the PSCs role in a crisis, risk management will always be linked to the lowest bidder. Whereas in the Western world one of the discussion points on the role of the PSCs is related to the fact that only those that can afford the private security services may take advantage of it, in China there is not yet a clear understanding of the value of reliable and professional security services. While macro differences arise from the employment of private security actor by the US government or the Chinese, one similarity is related to the recent Chinese trend of the 'revolving door', which is very common in the US private military and security sector (Amey 2004). As has happened since the 1990s between the US Army and the top echelons of several PSCs, China is also starting to experience a shift of personnel from the PLA and the PAP to the private security sector. In the United States, the phenomenon has reached a preoccupant dimension leading to a Senate investigation that pointed out how conflict of interests surfaced between former army and intelligence officials, their private sector employers and the public bidding system (Abrahamsen 2010). However, in China the novelty of the PSCs has not yet been put under the Communist Party anti-corruption department microscope. Nevertheless, considering the zealous nature of the anti-corruption campaign that has led to the decapitation of the PLA command and control structure since the early 2013, it is not improper to forecast closer attention to the subject in due course.

2.3 Chinese Own Perception of the Domestic and International Security Market

The first comprehensive industry report (PTT 2016) on the Chinese overseas security was published after the 13 March 2016 forum on overseas risk conference and security management held by the Phoenix think tank and the Tsinghua University in Beijing. The report is a first step by Chinese leading research centres to address specifically the future role of Chinese PSCs abroad. At the same time several leading Chinese think tanks such as Shanghai Academy of Social Sciences (SASS) and Shanghai Institute for International Studies (SIIS) or universities such as Fudan have taken into consideration the risk along the BRI (Shanghai Daily 2016) including the analysis on the role of the PSCs. The report presents a first assessment on the Chinese international enterprises' security management containing risk assessment, insurance management, overseas security and consular protection.

The Phoenix international think tank research group field analysis on the current situation of the Chinese market for force provides a glimpse on the Chinese own perception of the local PSCs weakness and strengths.

Quoting the think tank investigation results, the vast majority of Chinese PSCs' awareness and ability is still 'very weak'. The report's final considerations are quite interesting as the Chinese propaganda, with special reference to the security sector, is prone to underline only the strength minimizing any weakness. The report presents the imperative need of a more autonomous and capable private security industry. Without taking into account the arbitrary exclusion of some large Chinese PSCs and the inclusion of foreign security companies based in China that have a business model more oriented to security intelligence and risk assessment services, the results are still in line with the conclusions drawn by the several Western counterparts. Another commonality is the critique to the Chinese PSCs and SOEs to overstate Beijing's capabilities abroad, confiding in the Chinese government last minute support and rescue in case of need.

The list of perceived PSCs' weakness includes a broad range of neglected management capabilities. One of the most common missing capabilities is a professional security management team able to detail accurate budget request when bidding for a security contract overseas. The lack of international experience and exposure to the international security problems is well represented by unrealistic lower bidding. Therefore, inexpensive bids allow unknown Chinese PSCs to compete with more professional Chinese companies. Unfortunately, low bids do not face the real costs that the company is going to incur in operating in hostile territories. Consequently, shortcuts and budgetary constrictions are going to affect negatively an already-precarious situation.

Moreover, the competition for the lowest bidder deters an efficient growth of the local market for force, as the Chinese professional corporations that truly understand the project safety operating costs are going to be outbidden by amateurs. At the same time, the SOEs' lack of willingness to pay and understanding of the high-risk costs associated with some overseas projects allow the participation of unqualified operator. The lack of proper filters in the security bidding system solely based on pricing requirements are hurting the market itself, as it already happened during the last three decades in the provision of local security services in China. The informality of the Chinese market for force is deeply rooted in the business referral network in which SOEs and former Chinese police and army officials share long-term friendship, common interests and their local network of contacts. Therefore, the contracting procedure and the security project implementation are relying on the personal network of the Chinese PSCs' CEO than on their capability to bid for a project. Even when their competence is unquestioned, the chance to know that there is an open tender is quite narrow.

The Chinese Mainland private security market is starting only now to move from an informal and fragmented setting to a more mature sector where the Chinese state and private corporations begin to realize that their long-term monetary savings in contracting a professional's security company are going to surpass the amount of money spent on their services.

The central government and the Chinese enterprises associations from the China Council for the Promotion of International Trade (CCPIT) to the Chinese Contractors Association are already aware that the Chinese companies investing abroad are in desperate need of security management capabilities. The contracting system to find the proper private solution provider is still not clearly defined, and it does need a government intervention to define the proper selection and monitoring process. The government support in defining a proper monitoring system in the qualification of the Chinese PSCs is going to help most of the SOEs that do not possess in-house effective security management capabilities.

Today, the scale of China's overseas security market amounts to more than US$10 billion. However, the sector is affected by several development challenges that the Phoenix report summarizes as:

- Late start
- Too rapid development
- Overcoming challenges

The Chinese overseas security industry is perceived to have begun around 2004 with the killing of 11 Chinese workers in Afghanistan, during the building of a road in Kunduz (China Daily 2004). The Afghan crisis imposed a reality check in Beijing that has generated a series of policy documents promulgated to strength the capabilities as well as the responsibilities for the SOE workers' safety.

After 2004, several large SOEs began to invest in the overseas security capabilities at internal management level and in external security providers. Compared to the beginning of the modern private security industry in the 1960s and in the 1980s, the Phoenix think tank considers the Chinese market for force as a latecomer in the overseas security industry. The late start forced a steep learning pattern on the Chinese PSCs, in order to avoid the costly mistakes committed by the foreign counterparts during the last decades.

In spite of the late start, the Chinese market for force has witnessed a fast-pace growth due to overseas security needs driven by the BRI spread of investments.

Since 2013, the expansion of the Chinese overseas market for force has been constantly increasing, reaching a critical mass in 2015. According to the Chinese analysis, the market size reached US$10.3 billion with the energy SOEs security expenditure reaching US$2 billion per year (PTT 2016).

The overcoming challenges are still related not only to the complexity of overseas market for force but also to the fragmentation of the Chinese PSCs. The fast development of the market linked with a loose regulatory system is prone to abuses. The lack of accurate statistical data on the scope, size and capabilities of the Chinese PSCs operating abroad as well as the number of Chinese nationals involved in overseas security services is still negatively affecting an accurate market analysis. The lack of transparency in the budget allocation and in the bidding system is one of the several problems that affect the informal market for force. Additionally, the absence of proper filters to assess the Chinese PSCs' effective capabilities and the security officers' previous track record and experience adds constraints to the problem.

While Chinese security practitioners brag on the presence of hundreds of security companies that claim overseas security capabilities, the Phoenix's think tank reduces the number to 20. A more conservative estimate, in line with the international security companies' criteria, could even reduce this latter figure to a mere dozen.

During the last decade, the Chinese insurance industry sector progressively developed the risk management capabilities necessary to address the Chinese foreign direct investment (FDI) needs. Also, the pace of the Chinese insurance sector development in the comprehension of the market for force is speeding up.

The result of the survey carried on by the Phoenix think tank underlines how the Chinese security industry still recognizes two world-leading actors as an example to follow for the local PSCs. The company G4S and Control Risks started earlier to pitch their services and capabilities to the Chinese SOEs in dangerous areas of the globe and then they both established a presence in China in order to follow not only the Chinese SOEs but also the foreign companies investing in Mainland. The business operations localized in China, if not contracted by foreign companies with business intelligence and local security needs, mainly use the support of the mother company international network.

Most of the international PSCs localized in China are characterized by high standards and high fees and most of the time are able to acquire important share of the Chinese international security projects as several of the top Chinese PSCs subcontract to them the services in more sensible areas.

Specialized security publications as well as the mainstream media devoted more attention on how the Chinese companies can avoid massive losses through effective risk control and how the central government has to promote the safety of the citizen and enterprises abroad. The Chinese magazine *Security & Technology Protection* (2016) published a dedicated assessment on the main domestic security companies operating overseas. The assessment is quite interesting as it sheds light on the perception that the Chinese analysts have their own private security sector. Unfortunately the quantitative approach utilized lacks some arbitrary omissions as some leading international security companies registered as Chinese business entity are included while others with the same capabilities are missing. The assessment titled 'Fast Development and Big Challenges' scrutinizes the domestic security industry and the first steps of the Chinese PSCs operating abroad. The research is based on interviews, questionnaires and the information available online covering the typology of the security services provided, the PSC business footprint in other countries, the number of overseas branches, the company working history and field experience, and quite important details such as the percentage of the employees that are fluent in English and in the languages of the countries served. The assessment ranks the top ten Chinese PSCs operating abroad, and not surprisingly the first and second positions belong to two international PSCs: G4S and Control Risks. While G4S offers the security guard services, Control Risks is included in the list without taking into account that the company business model is evolving towards security and integrity risk consultancy.

Following are the third to the tenth places:

- Beijing Dewei Security Service Co. Ltd
- Zhongguo Anbao China Security Industry Co., Ltd
- Huaxin Zhongan (Beijing) Security Service Co., Ltd
- Shanghai Zhongchenwei Security Service Group Co. Ltd
- Beijing Dingtai Anyuan Guard & Technology Research Institute
- Shengzhen Zhongzhou Tewei Security Consultant Co. Ltd
- Beijing Guanan Security & Technology Co. Ltd
- Shandong Huawei Security Group Ltd Subsidiary

In every category of the assessment, G4S stands at the top with Control Risks following closely, while the other corporations lack substantially some of the key categories. The report underlines how compared to the international counterparts the domestic security companies have a lot to catch, lacking the experience that G4S has matured in the security services for decades and Control Risks that started in 1975. In comparison, the oldest Chinese PSCs started their first steps after 1993.

While the international PSCs are actively seeking new clients and chances to exploit new market, as the case of the BRI, the Chinese PSCs still count on the government-favourable policies to preserve their market position inside China. At the same time, the PSCs venturing abroad are looking exclusively to cooperate with Chinese companies and at this moment are not interested in pursuing foreign clients, with the exceptions of the ones that are already utilizing their services in Mainland.

Also comparing the incomes of the international top PSCs with the Chinese counterpart underlines the imbalance in the Chinese security market development equalled to the international playfield. A simple glance at the published accounting figures shows how the income of the biggest Chinese domestic security company reaches a fraction of the overseas one. Still quoting the assessment, the Chinese PSCs' service capabilities and the business models are still at the basic level and in their infancy. From the business angle, the Chinese private security industry lags behind due to several constraints including the market capacity that is not large enough to afford sophisticated services. Prior to the incoming revenue from the BRI, the lack of williness to pay for high level professionals has negatively affected the sector development. Most of the Chinese corporations that have started in the recent past to invest abroad, with noted exception in the natural resources sector, have done it in developed countries such as the European Union (EU), North America or Japan. Only recently, the majority of the Chinese companies, including private small- and medium-sized enterprises (SMEs), are looking to invest in high-risk countries.

The think tank assessment focus also shifts on the domestic and international guidelines provided by Beijing. Even though the country declared some policy and instruction on overseas security enhancement, the controlling organism interest is more related to the financial assessment requirements than the security ones. Also, several Chinese companies that are just subcontractor in a larger infrastructure construction project do have a limited profit margin, and in their business model the high cost associated with the provision of high-quality security service is considered unreasonable.

Considering that at least half of the BRI going out projects are related to engineering sub-contracting with narrow revenues, the market of high-level security could not tap a large amount of funds. The central government and the insurance companies felt the necessity to step in, raising the bar on the level of engineer companies that could operate abroad without incurring unnecessary risks just to maintain their limited profit margin. The current negative spillover in the security small market pool is related to the fact that it attracts the lowest level of security service providers that are used to employ personnel without any training or real capabilities besides sitting in a guard boot with a mobile phone playing video games or watching TV serials. While this model is still effective in Mainland China due the high-level security provided by the police, it is not the case aboard. The scale of the average Chinese PSCs is also a limitation not only in the capabilities to attract just sublevel labour force but also in the lack of international management capabilities. Several times the so-called bodyguards that were supposed to follow their VIP clients in overseas business trip were unable to apply for a foreign visa.[15]

The lack of business capability overseas is especially related to the threat assessment experience and the competence to cope strange with different social, political and regulatory environments. The Chinese PSCs operating overseas tend to lack the necessary connections and networking with the local government overlaying on the consular protection and the perception that Beijing government-to-government agreements could shield them from any trouble. Adding all the above-mentioned problems to the complete lack of local intelligence, supply chain management and logistical and legal support, it is just an invitation to future disasters.

The low level of internationalization and the lack of comprehensive capabilities are well expressed in the assessment report and in the forums on the BRI security. Unfortunately the market informal regulations and the lack of international oversight mechanism are not helping faster changes for better-quality services.

While China after three decades of business development has also shifted the policy approach from norm-taker to norm-maker, the Chinese PSCs going out along with the wave of Chinese FDIs are trend followers and not trendsetters. International security companies such as Control Risks are eager to find business opportunities in the global market offering innovative services and top-notch capabilities localized with the specific needs of the clients; on the contrary, Chinese PSCs depend mostly on Chinese clients.

Since Chinese PSCs lack the necessary language, intelligence gathering and diplomatic capability, most of their security forces can only function within the walls of the Chinese workers' gated compound, depending on external armed protection from local militia or international contractors. Without international cooperation and a broader vision on the provision of high-level business services, the Chinese private security industry is posed to remain a passive spectator in the overall BRI global development.

In accordance with the assessment and forum discussion results, the security industry must develop its own business capability, and the change does not have to exclusively affect the number of guards sent abroad or the number of contracting clients, but it has to have mature competences and attitudes. One of the urgent issues that the central government has to take into consideration is the standard required for cross-countries operations and management. While the ban in firearms handling for the Chinese nationals going abroad is seldom circumvented with acquisition of locally available automatic weapons, the backslash in case of collateral damages could be a serious problem not only for the PSCs involved but for the Chinese government efforts in maintaining the non-interference principle.

One of the steps that could accelerate the development of a more professional and international security industry is the cooperation not only with international PSCs and training/certifying organizations but also with vertical market integration that could increase the PSCs' capabilities. These kinds of vertical cooperation and strategic alliance are the ones established with international companies such as special insurance services (Hitchox, Integro) or with health insurance service providers such as International SOS. The mixing of insurance, healthcare and Chinese PSCs facing overseas risks constitutes an important learning platform to advance the overall Chinese security industrial sector. At the same time, considering how the Chinese security market is protected from external influence by the central government regulation, the main role in its reform is linked with Beijing will and not the free hand of the market. While even the Chinese analysts advocate more space to the market forces with respect to the government monopolistic approach, it is useful to remember how in the case of the US market for force the overall security sector expansion of $1 billion market per year has been driven most by the US government contracting.

2.4 From the *Anabasis* to the Online Security Apps

I say, therefore, that the arms with which a prince defends his state are either his own, or they are mercenaries, auxiliaries, or mixed. Mercenaries and auxiliaries are useless and dangerous; and if one holds his state based on these arms, he will stand neither firm nor safe; for they are disunited, ambitious and

> without discipline, unfaithful, valiant before friends, cowardly before enemies; they have neither the fear of God nor fidelity to men, and destruction is deferred only so long as the attack is; for in peace one is robbed by them, and in war by the enemy. The fact is, they have no other attraction or reason for keeping the field than a trifle of stipend, which is not sufficient to make them willing to die for you. *Macchiavelli: The Prince* Capt. 12th

Since the establishment of the Westphalia order and the birth of modern national armies, the image of the 'free lances' or the 'condottieri' has been increasingly negative. Nevertheless, today's PSCs are the modern reincarnation of a tendency that has its roots in ancient history. The practice of hiring soldiers to secure territories and properties or to participate in armed aggressions has existed since the time of the *Anabasis* (Xenophon 1998). In *Anabasis*, Xenophon narrates how in 401 BCE Cyrus the Younger employed a large army of Greek mercenaries to defeat his brother Artaxerxes II, in order to be crowned emperor of Persia. Alexander the Great of Macedonia contracted Greek mercenaries during his military expansion to the East. Mercenaries were able not only to increase the ranks of kings' and emperors' armies but also to provide special skills such as the Balearic Islands sling shooters who were contracted by Carthage to fight against Rome during the Punic wars. The Roman Empire was increasingly under pressure to guarantee a steady flow of recruits to the legions and to the border defence garrisons. Since the end of the fourth century, entire tribes of barbarians were contracted as autonomous militia (*foederati*) or embedded within the legions. A well-known example is drawn from the Varangian (Vikings), who were barbarian mercenaries that provided assault troops and the imperial guard during the Byzantine Empire.

During the Norman Conquest in England, Flemish mercenaries constituted an important part of William the Conqueror's army. Later on during the fragmentation of the Italian peninsula into a multitude of fiefdoms, the 'condottieri' were war chiefs who offered the skilled services of their armed men to the highest bidder.

During the end of the Middle Age, free companies composed of 'free lances' provided mercenary services to the city-states and kingdoms that needed armies during wartime but were not able to maintain them during peace time or during harvest time. The German free companies became famous for providing specialized combat services that the regular armies based on local conscription were not able to provide. At the end of the fifteenth century, Swiss Guard mercenaries competed with the Germans for the most effective men-at-arms that money could buy. The advancement of the hardware and tactics of warfare that occurred with the advent of the harquebus in the sixteenth century dented the Swiss monopoly over the privatization of violence, and the German 'landsknechts' became the most requested provider of mercenary services. During that period it was not uncommon to witness 'landsknechts' fighting on both sides of the conflict or switching sides to take up a better offer. It is not by chance that two of the most prominent thinkers of that period, Niccolò Machiavelli and Thomas More, expressed in their works a lengthy consideration on the role of mercenaries, albeit on opposite sides. In the *Prince*, Machiavelli warns against the employment of mercenaries, having witnessed personally how treacherous and ineffective it could be to employ soldiers motivated only by the coin. While in *Utopia*, More underlines how the professionalism of the barbarian mercenaries is a guarantee for the protection of the state.

During the Thirty Years' War, the role of mercenaries reached its apogee in Europe due to the demand for skilled practitioners of firearms and the need for constant drills and training in manoeuvring the forces. For example, over half of the casualties in the Battle of Lützen (1632) suffered by the army under the Swedish king Gustav II Adolf were German or other foreign mercenaries.

In Japan during the same historical period and until the Meiji era, skilled mercenaries played a significant role in turning battles into victories. While the Western perception is linked to fantasies and abundant literature on the Ninjas, several other mercenaries, such as the Saika Ikki, offered their services for the capable use of the harquebuses for a material reward.

During the American Revolution, German mercenaries were to be found on both sides of the battlefield. King George III of England's Royal Army included entire battalions from the German *land* Hesse-Kassel, known later on as 'Hessians'. The term 'Hessians' eventually became a generic term for German mercenaries that came from other principalities.

The national monopoly of force has been increasing since the seventeenth century, as the idea that national security should only be provided by the state with conscript national armies becomes a pillar of the modern statehood.

While the affirmation of the national armies during the nineteenth and twentieth centuries has cast a shadow on the utility of the private force, nevertheless the market outside the state monopoly of violence has been always present.

> Terrorism is not the only facet of contemporary conflict that is not new. Non-state actors, many of them in the business of war for personal profit, were features of medieval and early modern warfare: indeed the effort by seventeen-century European states to establish a monopoly on the use of armed force was in part a direct response to the suffering and destitution, the rape and pillage, wrought by competing freebooters, mercenaries and private military companies. (Strachan 2013)

Historical exceptions involve the positive role played by private chartered companies with a legal mandate to use force, granted by the respective governments. Examples range from the Portuguese, Holland's VOC and British Companies of the Indies where the state's monopoly on violence was contracted to chartered companies in order to protect holdings and monopoly rights from pirates and competitors. During that period, the positive attitude towards the use of private armies was justified by the necessity to protect investments that were far from the immediate reach of the state without incurring high costs of fixed garrisons. In this respect, even the British Army, until the late stages of the First World War, was smaller than that of other European counterparts. The British counted on a reduced contingent of trained volunteers to be deployed in the colonies and ready to fight small wars (Hart 1932).

In China, the negative connotation of the employment of private armies and mercenaries is rooted in modern national history. While the contempt for the mercenaries in the West dates back to the seventeenth century, in China it amounts to less than a century. From 1911 to 1930, the power vacuum left by the demise of the Qing imperial dynasty was filled by the rise of the warlords (Powell 2015). The Chinese saying of the 'Three Mores' well characterizes this period: 'More officers than soldiers, More soldiers than guns, More bandits than people' (Jowett 2013). The fall of the last imperial dynasty centralized power, accelerated by external pressures like the Sino Japanese conflict (1884–1895) as well as endogenous events such as the Boxer Rebellion (1900) (Fairbank, Liu, & Twitchett, Late Ch'ing, 1800–1911. Volume 11, Part 2 of The Cambridge History of China Series, 1980), ignited China's fragmentation in to provincial fiefdoms ruled by local military governors. The warlord era is commonly referred to as the time following the death of Yuan Shikai in 1916 and the fragmentation of the national army into hundreds of armed cliques ruled by warlords.

> According to Fung the political chaos surrounding the 1911 revolution and Yuan's rule brought about this notable change in the 'traditional civil-military' relationship, since the political power wielded by the warlords was never returned to the 'state bureaucracy', thus inaugurating an era marked by the 'ascendancy of the military'. (Ibidem)

The warlords ranged from small criminal gangs exercising limited power over a remote countryside area to regional armies that could count on an air force, artillery and armoured trains (Elleman 2001).[16] While several warlords attempted to gain imperial status by imposing their will over the rebellious provinces, none of them proved capable of the daunting task. An example is given by General Li Yuanhong, who managed twice, in 1922 and 1926, to get nominated as president of the newborn Chinese Republic but only for a limited time. Similarly, in 1926 the warlord Zhang Zuolin, who with the support of Japan managed to gain the control of the capital, was defeated just two years later by the Nationalists, led by generalissimo Jiang Jieshi (Chiang Kai-shek). The collapse of the central power and the surging uncertainty generated a rapid growth in armed men from half a million in 1916 to more than two million by the end of 1928.[17] The main armies of the time, referred as cliques, range from the Anhui clique, the United Northern Warlords clique, the Zhili clique, the Fengtian clique, the National People's Army and the National Revolutionary Army (NRA—Kuomintang). Each clique could count on a great number of men but only a fraction of them were well-armed veterans and capable officials. In order to supply soldiers, instructors, special weapons operators to control artillery or armoured trains, most of these armies engaged mercenaries from Russia, Japan and several other countries interested in providing weapons and materiel to the warring parties. In most cases, the pay for the warlords' armies was left to the soldiers themselves who looted the countryside after a victorious battle. Moreover, it was not uncommon to recruit bandits, adventurers and entire defeated armies as means to expand the quantity but not the quality of the armies. Therefore, the historical legacy of the warlord period has left a profound distrust in the private armies that is still a riddle in the common perception of freelance soldier.

Several power brokers were unscrupulous bandits who rose to power due to fortuitous circumstances, such as the case of Zhang Zongchang, the 'Dog Meat General'. In opposite cases, such as that of General Wu Peifu, the 'Scholar Warlords' were well-respected commanders. In both circumstances, the armies' weapons, which were provided by external sources, could comprise different types of equipment and a range of ammunition as well as foreign advisors and foreign mercenaries. Most of the mercenaries in the front-line troops were former Tsarist soldiers employed by Northern Chinese warlords, while Japanese, English, Czech and Italian specialists were employed in the major armies as general staff officials or skilled technicians. The 'Dog Meat' general employed more than 3000 White Russians and a personal guard composed of Cossack veterans. In contrast, the general Zhang Zuolin created a fighting foreign legion composed of 700 Russians and 300 Japanese. Russian and Japanese officers commanded each battalion.[18]

In addition to the small arms coming from all over the world, the warlords that were able to own an air force employed foreign pilots and foreign-made planes ranging from the Italian Ansaldo A30 to the Soviet R1 light bombers. During the warlord era, it was not uncommon to witness the transport plane German Junker A35 flown by Japanese pilots or the US instructors piloting the French Morane Saulnier 'Penguin' (Jowett 2013). The case of the White Russians distinguished themselves from the common perception of mercenaries, as several of them were driven not only by the coin but also by a strong anti-Bolshevik sentiment.

> This ideological aspect separated the White Russian mercenaries from the fifteen century Italian renaissance and the modern day Angolan meaning of a soldier of fortune who sought only monetary gain. (Chan 2010)

Also, the Chinese warlord era has its own share of foreign adventures that linked their name to the provision of war-related services. Francis 'One Arm' Sutton, an English adventurer who produced the Stokes mortar for several warlords, ended his mercenary career as major general for Zhang Zuolin. The Italian Amleto Vespa provided his services as a mercenary for the Northern clique and as a spy in Manchuria for the Japanese Empire.

In the late 1970s, Deng Xiaoping use of China's limited resources was focused on the economic development instead of financing the army modernization, promoting a double-digit GDP growth over 20 years. While three decades of peace dividends have permitted China to become leading economic power, the current geopolitical status quo imposes to the PLA new challenges that the army is not yet ready to face. This new dimension of the PLA's operational capabilities is deeply intertwined with China's economic leverage and growing diplomatic influence abroad. Currently, Beijing's long-term plan for the modernization of the PLA opens the door to several security providers that are upgrading both technical and training capabilities while providing overseas services that could not be tapped through official Chinese channels. Since 2015, control of the party over the PLA has been strengthened. The PLA's strategic aim has shifted from conventional combat capabilities to its ability to engage in short-term, high-intensity regional conflicts far from China's borders.[19] While the mainland PLA capabilities are growing, external instability and uncertainty require an immediate response. Moreover, China's expertise in sea lines of communication (SLOC) operations and the international anti-piracy mission is already reaching its maturity. In addition, disaster relief and UN peacekeeping missions are increasing steadily.

'China's expanding international economic interests are increasing demands for the PLAN to operate in more distant seas to protect Chinese citizens, investments and critical sea lines of communications (SLOC)'.[20]

Since 2015 the increased scope and volume of the Chinese ODI by Chinese international funds and multinationals with headquarters based in China have boosted the demand for more sophisticated security services. It is not uncommon to see Chinese managers looking intently at their mobile phone App to check on the latest news on worldwide security or to get an update on a specific area where the financial fund is investing, if the company is operating in increasing dangerous area, or if the managers are travelling in search of profitable deals in politically unstable regions.

2.5 From Africa's Bush Wars to Afghanistan: The Evolution of the Anti-mercenary Law

In the 1960s, during the African postcolonial wars, the role of private military companies reappeared with vengeance. In order to avoid the damages and unsettlement perpetrated by small but well-trained and armed mercenaries, the Additional Protocol I was added to the Geneva Convention in 1977.[21] A strict set of six parameters has to be met in order to define a 'mercenary'. A mercenary is defined as a person who:

1. Is specially recruited locally or abroad in order to fight in an armed conflict
2. Does, in fact, take a direct part in the hostilities

3. Is motivated to take part in the hostilities essentially by the desire for private gain and, in fact, is promised, by or on behalf of a party to the conflict, material compensation substantially in excess of that promised or paid to combatants of similar ranks and functions in the armed forces of that party
4. Is neither a national of a party to the conflict nor a resident of territory controlled by a party to the conflict
5. Is not a member of the armed forces of a party to the conflict
6. Has not been sent by a state which is not a party to the conflict on official duty as a member of its armed forces

In addition, rule 108[22] to the Additional Protocol I re-enforces that the mercenaries do not have the right to combatant or prisoner-of-war status. Since the 1960s, the United Nations (UN) has dedicated increasing attention to 'mercenary activities', underlining the need for better involvement in the interaction between states and other actors, attempting to regulate the modern private security services industry and to make business enterprises accountable in respecting human rights. In 1989, the UN released a draft set of regulations to control and limit the recruitment and employment of mercenaries. The same set of regulations then was ratified in 2001.[23]

A common critique of these definitions is that they are related to a specific area and historical period, for example the African postcolonial wars; therefore, it is not possible to adopt it in the modern context without appropriate modifications. The twentieth-century demand for private security forces widely differentiates the actors and the settings compared to the African postcolonial wars. Even the latest policy suggestions aimed to regulate the sector during the Afghan conflict were based not on local necessities but on the previous experiences matured in Iraq. Furthermore, the increased role of PMCs is still unquestioned by the international community that instead leaves regulation and enforcing to national and state domestic laws (Scheimer 2009). According to the Additional Protocol I and the Geneva Convention, the legal status of civilian contractors depends upon the nature of their work and their nationalities with respect to that of the combatant and to the fact that they do not take an active part in the conflict. Hence the contractors' non-combatant support role categorizes them as civilians who are entitled to protection under the Geneva Convention. Nevertheless, the definitions get blurred when the contractors bear arms in response to a direct or perceived threat or when they provide training that augments local offensive capabilities. Moreover, several countries including the United Stated and China did not ratify the previously mentioned UN resolution 44/34.

Today the process of political and economic globalization has led multinational companies, especially the ones related to energy and other natural resources extraction, to operate in international areas that are often unstable. In this regard, the PSCs fill the vacuum of power that weak states are not able secure with their police and military forces. Currently, from the Chinese side the narrative related to the growing private security industry is unrelated with the provision of military services or the provision of military equipment, as China is not actively engaged in a war since the 1979. Nevertheless, the search for talented local human resources is starting to tap into the growing number of Chinese military personnel who have overseas experience as UN envoys or have been appointed to diplomatic security details. Several articles on the subject mention the employment of contractors from the Snow Leopard PAP SWAT team[24] and the more secretive special forces units. The reality is that the pool of potential security personnel includes former Chinese military personnel who have been trained by the PAP with further private experience in the security department of oil and gas SOEs such as Poly Golden Concordia Group. Other contractors' experiences range from military training as counterterrorist officials during the 2008 Beijing Olympics in order to protect the athlete village, to martial art expert with several months of on-site experience in Iraq, albeit with no formal military training. In several occasions, the contractor's CV reveals that additional qualifications have been developed while on a private contract abroad, such as security driving certifications, CPR and combat wound treatment, honed for private employment from previous training as SWAT team in the autonomous province of Xinjiang, as high-level guard duty in the Central Military Commission (Diaoyutai) or as amphibious specialist during the Boao Asian forum.[25]

The conceptual evolution in the use of force requires the creation of new paradigms that are not yet understood by many nation states. At the same time, the provision of private security services is not a new phenomenon. Modern PSCs, however, evolved during the last two Iraq wars, are going to affect how economic power may be used to influence states and non-state actors. Another aspect that will draw much scrutiny to Chinese PSCs is the possibility of the pre-emptive use of force, an act that crosses the thin line between private security services and formal military force.

The legal boundaries between PSCs that provide security services and the ones that provide military force appear initially to be quite easy to define. It is important to remember, however, how PSC 'passive services' are aimed to transfer or enhance military capabilities and have to be considered as a potential military force multiplier. 'The delivery of such services involves civilian rending of expertise that, nonetheless, directly enhances the recipient's military and security capabilities. All the services on offer by the private military industry have a direct impact on and contribute to the management of state's monopoly of legitimate violence' (Ortiz 2007). The case of Military Professional Resources Inc. (MPRI) in the former Yugoslavia exemplifies how the combat enhancing services could alter a conflict outcome. In 1994, the US State Department contracted MPRI to improve the Croatian army's fighting capabilities against the Serbs. In 1995, the Croatian army launched Operation Storm to liberate the self-proclaimed Serbian autonomous region of Krajina. Croatia's swift and surprising victory forced the Serbs to the negotiating table by the end of the same year (Avant, The Market for Force: The Consequences of Privatizing Security, 2005).

Nevertheless, it is quite unlikely that China is going to see the growth of its own version of infamous PSCs such as Executive Outcomes (EO) or Sandline. In the 1990s, the South African company EO, which became the paradigm for the provision of highly trained mercenaries, was rewarded by corporations that were profiting from the Angola and Sierra Leone civil wars. Similarly, Sandline—a UK company with links to EO—provided direct combat personnel to support the Papua New Guinea government's efforts against rebels. In both cases, the small but efficient employment of highly trained mercenaries operating advanced hardware and tactics enabled the local governments to overcome the opposing forces. Even air support was provided, with EO deploying a privately owned Russian Mi-24 Hind attack helicopter (Pelton 2006).

Since the second Iraqi conflict, the role of non-state entities has been characterized by the strategic and operational deployment of PSCs thanks, in part, to the blurring of international borders, as well as the role of central governments and private corporations. While the legal grey areas are increasing, the security vacuum has been filled by a growing number of PSCs that have evolved their services according to the market needs, from passive armed security to armed logistics that includes transfer of military equipment. Both wars in Iraq and Afghanistan, albeit in different conditions, saw the insurgents' cancer metastasize while war costs reached almost US$5 trillion.[26] Therefore the United States, which is fighting multiple conflicts in the condition of 'Perpetual War',[27] is not able to supply enough 'soldiers, diplomats or intelligence officers who are fluent in such languages as Arabic, Farsi, Pashto and Urdu … After its Post Cold war downsizing, the US military lacked enough troops to control both Afghanistan and Iraq, so the Pentagon relied heavily on contractors for everything' (Boot 2014).

A senior European diplomat who has been tracking the employment of contractors during the Afghan conflict has summarized the privatization of violence in one succinct sentence: 'While I was boarding a military plane leaving Kabul, I saw this bunch of bearded men, sporting trendy sunglasses and a wide array of weapons. The scene reminded me of the Manzoni bravoes.'[28]

2.6 Lack of Definition, Accountability and Transparency

> In the councils of government, we must guard against the acquisition of unwarranted influence, whether sought or unsought, by the military-industrial complex. The potential for the disastrous rise of misplaced power exists, and will persist. 17 January 1961, US President Dwight Eisenhower

One of the problems that affect academic research in the PSC field is the lack of primary source data. The absence of transparency that surrounds the role of the PSC, whether the protection granted by the state or the inability to trace international money transfers, or the complacency of governments that turn Nelson's eye to the problem, all of this makes it very hard to check sources and verify facts. Nonetheless, the abuse in the academic narrative of second-hand information, which is erroneously treated as primary source, generates myths that start to have their own life. On a couple of occasions during international workshops on Chinese security corporations, the number of Russian PSCs active in Hong Kong has skyrocketed to dozens of new firms that are added to the total at each new workshop. The trend started with some quotes by a Chinese scholar who had 'heard' during the 2015 Valdai Club forum that the number of Russian contractors in Hong Kong was increasing. While it is not news that Hong Kong is one of the favourable locations to register an offshore company, most of the Russian PSCs prefer Cyprus or Dubai to settle their offshore accounts. Also, most of the firms registered in Hong Kong just use an offshore virtual office and a banking account in order to avoid the Russian regulators and to deal with the problems associated with transferring large sum of money in light of the sanctions on Russia and the monitoring of SWIFT transactions (Forbes 2015). Nevertheless, the narrative of an annual double-digit increase of Russian PSCs with actual offices and personnel in Hong Kong has been presented as hard data during several academic workshops on PSCs. Official data on Hong Kong as hub for Russian PSCs emerged in the 2012 with the case of Moran Security, a Russian PMC registered in Saint Petersburg. A subsequent investigation by Denis Korotkov,[29] a reporter for *Fontanka*, discovered that the Hong Kong registration was related only to an offshore address established for financial purposes. The Russian criminal code Article 359 (1996) defines and outlaws soldiers of fortune activity. A recent amendment of the Article 208 in 2013 was made in order to outlaw the participation of Russian citizens in armed conflict without the payment of a salary. This move was not related to further restrict the role of mercenaries but to find legal grounds to prosecute the increasing flow of jihadists moving from the Caucasus to Syria to increase the ranks of IS. Also, the case of the Russian PSC, which is registered in Hong Kong under the name Slavonic Corps Ltd, is related to the Syrian conflict. The company allegedly provided support for President Bashar al-Assad through Russian contractors. In October 2013, the jihadi website Kavkaz Center posted the documents of a Russian contractor killed in a skirmish near the city of Homs. In this case the contractor, employed by Slavonic Corp and subcontracted by Moran Security Group, a Moscow-based PMSC, turned out to be alive and well in Russia. Besides being wrong on the death of the Russian contractor, the news sparked a series of investigations on the claims that Russian mercenaries were operating in Syria to protect Assad's regime. A series of reports by *Fontanka's* journalist discovered that Moran president Vyacheslav Kalashikov, a reservist lieutenant colonel from the Federal Security Service of the Russian Federation (FSB), had subcontracted Slavonic Corp to provide 267 Russian battle-ready contractors in an effort to stop the anti-Assad rebels. Following the return of the contractors to Russia after a failed attempt to regain the area East of Palmyra from IS fighters, the FSB temporarily detained the men for questioning and subsequently arrested Vadim Gusev, vice president of Moran, under the Article 359 of the Criminal Law that forbids the recruitment of mercenaries. In this respect the plausible deniability provided by the employment of a private corporation has worked fine for the Russian Federation in order to openly deny its open support for Assad. Rejecting the operational role provided by private companies such as Moran and Slavonic allowed the Russian government to avoid an international incident until open support for the Assad regime began with the start of the aerial bombing campaign.

From the journalistic point of view, interest in this field has grown sharply since the Nisour Square incident that precipitated the demise of the American PSC Blackwater. Unfortunately, most of the accounts, which tend to be inflated by hyperbole, depict the employment of private contractors as 'Soldier of Fortune', 'Dog of Wars', 'Licensed to Kill' or 'Soldier of Misfortune'. This approach deforms research into the private security sector.

Since the beginning of warfare, the role of private armies has been related to the commodification of conflict. In a smaller-scale format compared to the PMCs, the PSCs' 'killing potential' is the insurance that protects their client's assets, whether workers or infrastructure. As in the case of an army, PSCs' use of force is focused primarily on deterrence and only in the last instance on its use. The lesson drawn from the Pentagon during the Iraq and Afghanistan conflicts is that over-reliance on contractors does not automatically promote efficiency or cost savings compared to the public sector. At the same time, the assertiveness of the armed contractors hindered efforts to win the hearts and minds of the population. Contractors' armoured convoys transporting VIPs or DOD materiel at high velocity through the troubled streets of Bagdad or Kabul while firing weapons to avoid proximity with oncoming vehicles may have made logistical and security sense. While achieving their objective in this manner, however, the contractors missed the broader picture of post-conflict state building by failing to abide by the same rules of engagements that applied to uniformed personnel.

The security vacuum filled by the provision of private security services urgently revealed the need for a clear and mutually agreed definition of what is mercenary in contrast to passive security. The Chinese market for force currently does not require the full range of services—such as armed response, armed aviation, military logistic and prisoner interrogation—that were developed during the latest US-led conflict. Nevertheless, examples drawn from Iraq and Afghanistan may be used to avoid repeating the same mistakes during the evolution of the Chinese market for force. PSC personnel include armed contractors that cannot be defined as civilians' military personnel even though they are embedded in a military structure. The Chinese case is more similar with the Iraq American contracting company AISG than with Blackwater. AISG (Andress 2007) was created in Iraq as a local private security start-up consisting of former Custer Battle personnel backed by Iraqi financiers. AISG provided construction and logistical services to the US stabilization effort using a 'flying below radar' approach that avoided heavy armoured convoys and highly visible contractors. Employing mainly Kurdish Peshmerga and other local talent backed up by American specialists ranging from former military personnel and engineers, AISG managed a more subtle approach in dealing with local threats. At the same time, the company's construction workers operating in the Iraqi insurgent areas experienced the same threats and risks faced by the coalition soldiers: insurgent attacks, improvised explosive devices (IEDs) and suicide bombings. In the AISG case, it is quite straightforward that the company's contractors cannot be defined as mercenaries according to the UN definition. While AISG's main contracts were related to infrastructure construction such us the set-up of IT networks or worksite management, they had to rely on armed personnel. Also, during the company activities in Iraq, several employee died by insurgent fire. While operating under contract to the US government, companies such as AISG operated in a legal limbo between local laws and regulations, the international regulations and the law that applied to the contracting agencies that were part of the US stabilization effort and under the jurisdiction of the US government and the US Army.

On November 2010, an investigation commissioned by the UN and produced by Global Research (Prado 2016) underlined the main pitfalls regarding the use of private contractors as follows:

> [T]hey pose a threat to civilians and to international human rights law. … The negative impact of the activities of "private contractors", "private soldiers", or "guns for hire" whatever denomination we might choose to name the individuals employed by a private military and security companies as civilians but in generally heavily armed. In the cluster of human right violations allegedly perpetrated by employees of these companies which the Working Group has examined once can find: summary executions, acts of torture, cases of arbitrary detention … It also appear that PMSCs, in their search for profit, neglected security and do not provide their employees with their basic rights, and often put their staff in situations of danger and vulnerability.

From a more Sino-centred point of view, the historical legacy of Chinese warlords has left a profound mistrust over the entire concept of private soldiering of any kind. Therefore, it is not difficult to forecast that significant constraints will be placed against leading Chinese PSCs as they seek to increase their operational capabilities, especially if those PSCs have exclusive links with top national SOEs. This would be essential in order to avoid SOEs pursuing their own interests that are not fine-tuned with national interests (Liu 2010). At the same time, it will be quite challenging for Beijing to control the SOEs' outbound investments and operations, especially those related to the flow of money between overseas accounts. In this case, the PSCs could benefit from SOEs' capital accounts located outside the reach of the People's Bank of China. The new economic footprint over the BRI put China in a position of dire need for PSCs, while at the same time the new trends in localized high-intensity conflicts and counterterrorism have shifted the modern armies' operational needs towards increased reliance on special operation forces, airpower, kinetic drone missions and intelligence gathering. While Chinese needs are related to qualified manpower shortages, Western armies continue to perceive the role of contractors as a viable alternative to put regular boots on the ground with the air support and surgical strikes by special forces.

Notes

1. The International Code of Conduct Association under the omen of the Swiss government established in the 2010, a regulatory framework as part of the Montreux in order to standardize the PMSCs.
2. http://icoca.ch/sites/all/themes/icoca/assets/icoc_chinese3.pdf
3. Beijing Yindun Security Services Co. Ltd., Huawei International Security Services Co. Ltd. and Hua Xin Zhong An Security Services (Beijing).
4. http://icoca.ch/
5. The central government plans budget for 2015 public security amounts to 154.2 billion yuan ($24.6 billion) according to a Finance Ministry report distributed Thursday before the start of the annual session of the National People's Congress.
6. Regulation on the Administration of Security and Guarding Services, adopted in 2009 via State Council Order No. 564, Article 1. English translation http://www.lawinfochina.com/display.aspx?lib=law&id=7779
7. Ibid. Article 8.
8. Ibid. Article 45.
9. Regulation on the Administration of Use of Guns by Full-time Guards and Escorts Decree adopted in 2002 via No. 356 of the State Council of the People's Republic of China, English translation http://www.lawinfochina.com/Display.aspx?lib=law&Cgid=40814

10. Australian Department of Foreign Affairs and Trade archives: http://foreignminister.gov.au/releases/2009/fa-s090709.html
11. American Security Company
founded in 1997 as Blackwater USA, providing security services ranging from training to private military, was renamed Xe Services in 2009 and has been sold and rebranded as Academi in 2011. Subsequently, Academi has been acquired by Constellis Holding also owner of a similar PMC, Triple Canopy.
12. In the year 2007 in Baghdad, 17 Iraqi civilians are shot dead by Blackwater's contractors covering an armoured convoy. At the end of 2014, the US Federal district court convicted four of the contractors for murder, manslaughter and weapons charges.
13. 'Baptized in its modern form after the 1991 Gulf War, the hybrid threat construct is a sophisticated amalgam of unrestricted threat activities that have resisted codification and generated a labyrinth of contradictory explanation. The hybrid concept bypasses the cognitive boundaries of traditional threat characterization and the application of organized collective violence' (Major Brian P. Fleming, U.S. Army 2011).
14. Rupert Smith 'The Utility of Force. The Art of War in the Modern World' 2006 Penguin.
15. Interview with Chinese Contractors Association Beijing in November 2015 (disambiguation: the term 'contractor' in this association is related to the contractors involved in infrastructure projects and related subcontracting and not exclusively to security contractors).
16. The Chinese army during the 1920s was remarkably well armed and equipped. Bruce Elleman 'Modern Chinese Warfare, 1795–1989' Warfare and History Routledge 2001.
17. '... from about 500,000 in 1916 to 700,000 a year later. By 1922, when the major war began there were 1.2 million men under arms ... in the 1925 this figure had risen to 1.4 million. As the fighting between Nationalists and the Northern Warlords began in earnest in 1926 this figure has risen to 1.6 million and it reached more than 2 million by the end of those campaigns.' Philip Jowett 'Chinese Warlord Armies 1911–1930' (2010) Osprey Publishing.
18. Ibid.
19. Department of Defense United States of America, Annual Report to Congress 'Military and Security Developments Involving the People's Republic of China 2016' April 26, 2016.
20. Ibid.
21. Article 47 of Protocol Additional to the Geneva Conventions of 12 August 1949, and relating to the Protection of Victims of International Armed Conflicts (Protocol I).

22. International Committee of the Red Cross (ICRC). Rule 108. https://ihldatabases.icrc.org/customary-ihl/eng/docs/v1_rul_rule108
23. International Convention against the Recruitment, Use, Financing and Training of Mercenaries art. 1, December 4, 1989, 2163 U.N.T.S. 75; also UN Secretary General Ban Ki-moon's address to urgently review its use of mercenaries to carry out security and peacekeeping work ahead of the 2013 General Assembly. 'UN Unions believe this practice is damaging the UN and putting staff at increasing risk, and taking place against the worrying backdrop of an attack on staff employment rights by UN management.' http://staffcoordinatingcouncil.org/attachments/article/191/UN%20report%20working%20group%20mercenaries.pdf
24. 'They also seemed to have captured the attention of the wider Chinese populace; one blog post reposted in a Global Times article called by name for the Snow Leopards to be sent to Sudan to rescue a group of 29 kidnapped Chinese.' https://jamestown.org/program/assessing-chinas-response-options-to-kidnappings-abroad/#sthash.vYSZ3knS.dpuf, see also Global Time 'Trained and untamed: China's elite Snow Leopard Commandos' April 8, 2015. http://www.globaltimes.cn/content/915758.shtml
25. Summary of Chinese PSCs' CV personnel provided by a Chinese recruiter specialized in providing former Chinese army officers to the Chinese PSCs (Shanghai, December 2016).
26. http://watson.brown.edu/costsofwar/
27. 'The United States has entered an era of perpetual war. The U.S. military has been at war for 15 straight years with no end in sight, and President Obama will soon have the dubious distinction of being the only American president to have been at war for all eight years of a two-term presidency. The traditional logic of American wars—that the United States would mobilize, fight, win, and end its wars through overwhelming force of arms—no longer seems to apply. Today's wars can be characterized more as conflicts in the grey zone, ambiguous battles with less-defined shapes and even less-clear outcomes. This increasingly blurred line between peace and war is posing a range of new challenges for the U.S. military, for elected officials, and for the nation as a whole.' David W. Barno and Nora Bensahel 'Fighting and winning in the "gray zone"' May 19, 2015. http://warontherocks.com/2015/05/fighting-and-winning-in-the-gray-zone/
28. 'The bravoes/bravi were mercenaries engaged by local lords in Italy during the sixteenth and seventeenth century, they use to display flamboyant dress and aggressive behaviours.' Shanghai, informal discussion with senior European diplomat previously posted in Afghanistan (November 2016).
29. St Petersburg Send Contractors to Syria (November 15, 2013). http://www.interpretermag.com/st-petersburg-sends-contractors-to-syria/

References

Abrahamsen, R. 2010. *Security Beyond the State: Private Security in International Politics*. Cambridge: Cambridge University Press.

Amey, S.H. 2004. *The Politics of Contracting*. Project On Government Oversight (POGO), June 29. http://www.pogo.org/our-work/reports/2004/gc-rd-20040629.html. Accessed 2015.

Andress, C. 2007. *Contractor Combatants: Tales of an Imbedded Capitalism*. Nashville, TN: Thomas Nelson Publishing.

Andrew Ericson, G.C. 2012. Enter China's Security Firms Chinese Private Security Companies Are Seeing an Opportunity as the U.S. Withdraws Troops from Iraq and Afghanistan. But plenty of Complications Await them. *The Diplomat*, February 21. http://thediplomat.com/2012/02/ente. Accessed 2015.

Avant, D.D. 2005. *The Market for Force: The Consequences of Privatizing Security, Cambridge University Press*. Cambridge.

Boot, M. 2014. More Small Wars. Counterinsurgency Is Here to Stay. *Foreign Affairs*, Number 6 November/December.

Chan, A.B. 2010. *Arming the Chinese: The Western Armaments Trade in Warlord China, 1920–28*. Vancouver: UBC Press.

China Daily. 2004. Eleven Chinese Workers Killed in Afghan Attack. *China Daily*, June 10. http://www.chinadaily.com.cn/english/doc/2004-06/10/content_338324.htm. Accessed 2016.

Elleman, B. 2001. *Modern Chinese Warfare, 1795–1989*. New York: Routledge.

Fairbank, J.K., K.-C. Liu, and D.C. Twitchett. 1980. *Late Ch'ing, 1800–1911. Volume 11, Part 2 of The Cambridge History of China Series*. Cambridge: Cambridge University Press.

Forbes. 2015. Russia to Retaliate if Bank's Given SWIFT Kick. *Forbes*, January 27. http://www.forbes.com/sites/kenrapoza/2015/01/27/russia-to-retaliate-if-banks-given-swift-kick/#5350dfa576df. Accessed 2016.

Gray, C.H. 1997. *Postmodern War*. London: Routledge.

Gray, C.S. 2009. *Chapter 10: Small Wars and Other Savage Violence*. Oxford: Oxford University Press.

GSA. 2008. *Division A: Department of Defense Authorizations*. Public Law No: 110–181, January 28. http://www.gsa.gov/portal/mediaId/184487/fileName/National_Defense_Authorization_Act_2008.action. Accessed 2017.

Hart, B.H. 1932. *The British Way in Warfare*. London: Faber.

Jowett, P. 2013. *China's Wars: Rousing the Dragon 1894–1949*. Oxford: Osprey Publishing.

Liu, H. 2010. Leashing the Corporate Dogs of War: The Legal Implications of the Modern Private Military Company. *Journal of Conflict & Security Law* 15: 167–168.

Molly Dunigan, U.P. 2015. *The Markets for Force. Privatization of Security Across World Regions*. Philadelphia, PA: University of Pennsylvania Press.

NATO. 2016. On Deterrence: … After the Fall of the Berlin Wall, a Long Period of Denial of Deterrence Followed. The Alliance Dramatically Downsized Its Forces (Conventional and Nuclear) and Persistently Reduced Defence Spending. *NATO Review Magazine*. http://www.nato.int/docu/review/2016/Also-in-2016/nato-deterrence-defence-alliance/EN/index.htm?utm_source=twitter&utm_medium=smc

Ortiz, C. 2007. The Private Military Company: An Entity at the Center of Overlapping Spheres of Commercial Activity and Responsibility. In *Private Military and Security Companies. Chances, Problems, Pitfalls and Prospect*, ed. Thomas Jäger and Gerhard Kümmel. Leiben: VS Verlag.

Parello-Plesner, J., and M. Duchâtel. 2015. *China's Strong Arm: Protecting Citizens and Assets Abroad*. London: Routledge.

Pelton, R.Y. 2006. *Licensed to Kill, Hired Guns in the War on Terror*. New York: Crown.

Powell, R.L. 2015. *Rise of the Chinese Military Power*. Princeton, NJ: Princeton University Press.

Prado, J.L. 2016. *The Privatisation of War: Mercenaries, Private Militaries and Security Companies (PMSC)*. Global Research, 9 April 2016 and U.N. Working Group on Mercenaries and Global Research.

PTT. 2016. *Phoenix International Think Tank*. 检索来源: Haiwai anquan guangli baogao (Overseas Security Management Report). http://pit.ifeng.com/event/special/haiwaianquanguanlibaogao/

PWC. 2016. Global State of Information Security Survey. *PwC Global*, October. https://www.pwc.com/sg/en/risk-assurance/assets/gsiss/global-state-of-information-security-survey-2017-sg.pdf

Scheimer, M. 2009. Separating Private Military Companies from Illegal Mercenaries in International Law: Proposing an International Convention for Legitimate Military and Security Support the Reflects Customary International Law. *American University International Law Review* 24 (6): 3.

Security & Technology Protection. 2016. *Bao An Yu Jishu*, July.

Shanghai Daily. 2016. Collaboration in Policy-making Urged for the Belt and Road' Initiative. *Shanghai Daily*, November 18. Accessed 2016.

Singer, P.W. 2003. *Corporate Warriors: The Rise of the Private Military Industry*. Ithaca: Cornell University press.

Smith, R. 2006. *The Utility of Force. The Art of War in the Modern World*. London: Penguin.

Strachan, H. 2013. *The Direction of War. Contemporary Strategy in Historical Perspective*. New York: Cambridge University Press.

'The Chinese Army During the 1920s were Remarkably Well Armed and Equipped' Bruce Elleman 'Modern Chinese Warfare, 1795–1989'. 2001. Warfare and History Routledge.

UNTS. 1989. *International Convention Against the Recruitment, Use, Financing and Training of Mercenaries Art. 1.* U.N.T.S. Art. 1, December 4.

Xenophon. 1998. *Xenophon 'Anabasi'.* Trans. by C.L. Brownson in Loeb Xenofon Classical Library Vol. III. Harvard University Press.

Xie Wenting 'Chinese Security Companies in Great Demand as Overseas Investment Surges' June 23, 2. h. 2016. Chinese Security Companies in Great Demand as Overseas Investment Surges. *Global Times*, June 23. http://www.globaltimes.cn/content/990161.shtml. Accessed 2016.

Xin, L. 2015. Private Security Companies Struggle to go Abroad Due to Legal Restrictions. *Global Times*, December 23. http://www.globaltimes.cn/content/960208.shtml. Accessed 2016.

Xin Hua. 2015. Chinese President Strongly Condemns Mali Hotel Attack. *Xin Hua Net*, November 21. http://news.xinhuanet.com/english/2015-11/21/c_134840105.htm. Accessed 2016.

CHAPTER 3

Protecting Chinese Overseas Interests

Abstract The Silk Road historical legacy legitimizes China's Belt and Road Initiative (BRI) as a pure commercial endeavour that is not related to hegemonic strategy. The overall Belt and Road footprint has already witnessed several incidents due to a lack of corporate social responsibilities (CSRs), as well as the absence of policies devoted to avoiding environmental degradation, work-related accidents and corruption. These kinds of incidents have fomented tensions that resulted in confrontation between Chinese and local workers. Today's global insecurity, ranging from terrorist threats to hybrid conflicts led by non-state actors, demands immediate policy responses. In this respect, it is imperative to address the normative approach to regulate the scope of the private security companies (PSCs) in light of new risks and security needs.

Keywords Silk Road • Hybrid conflict • Mercenaries • BRI security

3.1 The Silk Road: Modern Solutions for Ancient Problems

> This expansion of China horizons linked Asia together. These networks had hitherto been blocked by the Yuezhi and above all the Xiongnu, nomadic tribes who like the Scythians in Central Asia were a source of constant concern but were also important trading partners for livestock (...). (Peter Frankopan, *The Silk Roads. A New History of the World*)

© The Author(s) 2018

A. Arduino, *China's Private Army*,
https://doi.org/10.1007/978-981-10-7215-4_3

The Silk Road historical legacy legitimizes China's Belt and Road Initiative (BRI) as a pure commercial endeavour that is not related to hegemonic strategy. At the same time, the maritime and land route that crossed multiple Silk Roads during the most recent centuries have been plagued by security threats ranging from pirate incursions to attacks by nomadic tribes. The BRI's modern caravansaries are the rail networks and ports that China is building in order to fill Asia's US$8 trillion infrastructure gap.

Therefore, Chinese overseas interests are changing the decades-old principle of non-interference. The overall BRI footprint has already witnessed several incidents due to a lack of corporate social responsibilities (CSRs), as well as the absence of policies devoted to avoiding environmental degradation, work-related accidents and corruption. These kinds of incidents have fomented tensions that resulted in confrontation between Chinese and local workers. Until 2016, financial risk was the only perceived challenge to the BRI, while criminal and political violence have been overlooked. Oversight and management structures need to be set in place. In addition, lessons drawn by the United States from the use of private security companies (PSCs) could be adapted to the Chinese circumstances in order to avoid costly miscalculations.

The revival of the ancient Silk Road economic belt, as well as the network of the twenty-first-century maritime road, is aimed to enhance global connectivity and commercial activity. In modern times, the image of the old Silk Road has been built on the stereotype of caravans moving silk and spices from the East to the West. The Silk Road dream is conjured on the idea of bazaars, traders and camels flowing through such exotic cities as Bukhara and Samarkand from the Chinese city of Xi'an. Goods reached the final customers after the more than 8000 km route through northern India, Central Asia, the Parthia Empire, arriving at the far eastern borders of the Roman Empire. At that time silk was not the only exported good: spices, porcelain, oils and luxury goods made up the core of a flourishing market.

While the imperial Chinese and the bazaars along the Silk Road capitalized on the commercial network, the flow of wealth attracted predators in the form of bandits and better-organized criminal groups, as well as mustered mercenaries in its defence. The caravansaries along the road acted not only as storage facilities and restorative stopovers for the merchants, but also as beacons for adventurers and professional soldiers selling their lances to the highest bidder.

During the later Middle age, the European shift to mercantilism through sea lanes decreased the volume and the value of goods traded overland. At the same time, the need for anti-piracy activities in securing the trade lines increased. The renewed interest in the Eurasian land routes started with the demise of the Soviet Union. Central Asia's oil and gas resources attracted global and regional powers eager to exploit the abundance of natural resources. Since the 1990s, several narratives about the revival of the Silk Road have been proposed, from the New Silk Road Initiative stemming from the United States and Europe, the Iron Silk Road from Russia, as well as the Chinese-led revival of the Silk Road economic belt. Thanks to the astonishing financial resources that have been committed, the Chinese BRI leadership is now globally recognized as the leading initiative in the area. The BRI comprises the land belt and the maritime road fostering new links between Europe, East Asia, Middle East, South Asia and Eurasia. The Chinese efforts in promoting 'connectivity' are aimed to fill in Asia's US$8 trillion infrastructure gap (Cainey 2016). While most of the BRI detractors criticize the fact the BRI lacks a detailed blueprint, Beijing prefers not to present a strategy, but an initiative in order to avoid the perception of hegemonic power. Beijing's soft power, using the metaphor of a New Silk Road that connects China and the world, aims to mitigate worries that China's rise should be regarded as a threat.

Today, the modern caravansaries are the rail networks and ports along the BRI. The new network hubs, like the ancient stopovers, link trade routes and enable a constant flow of goods. Following the economic stagnation ignited by the US subprime mortgage crisis in 2008, China is promising enhanced trade and the capital to develop modern connectivity. Focusing purely on economic and commercial point of views, most of the states along the BRI are trying to acquire a bigger percentage of the Chinese outbound investments. At the same time, as had happened in the past history of the Silk Road, the sudden influx of wealth is generating new threats and risks. Nowadays, the peculiar geostrategic and geoeconomic features of the BRI, from Central Asia to Pakistan or alongside the Somali coast and the Malacca strait, are characterized by a high level of insecurity.

Again, one solution in the protection of the modern-age caravansaries from criminal and political violence could be found in PSCs.

While the Iraq and Afghanistan conflicts have reignited the hype on the PSCs, with the exponential increase in capital and manpower contracted to the war efforts, the BRI's need for security will not demand the same financial support. In this respect, it is still too early to witness a new golden age for the private market of force. The values of the PSC services contracted along the BRI would be a fraction of the hundreds of billions of dollars disbursed on yearly basis by the US-led coalitions in the recent conflicts. In this respect, the Chinese investments along the more troubled areas of the BRI have not yet been implemented, and are only a bad omen for the security issues to arise in the future. Nevertheless, several states that are crossed by the BRI are affected by insecurity and volatile political conditions. Consequently, the new entrepreneurial growth of private security contractors poses to fill the demand to support the state-owned enterprises' (SOEs) infrastructure-building process. Therefore, the private provision of security, intelligence and logistical services is a commodity in the New Silk Road market in and of itself. The lack of willingness to pay for sophisticated security services by Chinese SOEs is also related to the fact that more than half of the BRI project is related to infrastructure building. While the Chinese SEOs' capacity to build power plants, highways and railroads is unmatched, the project construction subcontracting to smaller Chinese firms implicates very narrow profit margins, limiting the capital that can be devoted to the provision of security services.

3.2 Belt and Road Initiative Risk Mapping

Today's global insecurity, ranging from terrorist threats to hybrid conflicts led by non-state actors, demands immediate policy responses. In this respect, it is imperative to address the normative approach to regulate the scope of the PSCs in light of the new risks and security needs.

On the Chinese side, the main focus on risk is still largely devoted to the financial viability of the projects. In this respect, Chinese law has evolved very quickly, specifying how the Chinese SOEs investing abroad have to avoid and manage financial risks.

The Chinese National Development and Research Commission (NDRC) defines in detail the conditions for overseas investment in the document on 'Interim Authorization Criteria for Overseas Investments' (2004), but the security threats that the Chinese SOEs are going to face outside Mainland China are still overlooked.

A recent example is seen in the total lack of geopolitical risk insurance for Chinese investments in Libya. At the height of the Muammar Gadhafi regime, Chinese contract projects in the area surpassed US$20 billion and the total sum insured and recovered after the fall of Gaddafi regime was just few million US dollars.[1]

Beijing exercises supervisory rights over the SOEs through the State-owned Assets Supervision and Administration Commission (SASAC) of the State Council, which in 2011 produced new risk control measures.[2] Although the SASAC maintains a supervisory role, most of the decision-making power is still vested in the SOEs' internal structure and several layers of byzantine bureaucracy, shielding the management from an effective supervision by the government's controlling bodies. Therefore, the SOEs are able to develop independent overseas investment strategies with the only requirement being to include a summary in their annual investment plans. The mandatory regulatory approvals include not only the NDRC but also the Ministry of Commerce (MOFCOM), increasing uncertainty about who the leading controlling government body is. Moreover, additional regulatory approval from SASAC is required if the overseas investment differs from the primary business scope of the SOE. Unfortunately, risk assessment and mitigation is overly focused on the financial part of the projects, due to the fact that the Chinese corporations have not been exposed in the mainland to the level of violence that they are going to face abroad. SOEs are used to employing Chinese workers in their overseas projects, and are prone to consider overseas working conditions to be exactly as in China. In cases of worker disputes or external problems, they are accustomed to swift support from the central government; along the BRI this will not be the case.

The BRI encompasses over 60 countries, differentiating broadly in local conditions. In this respect, the tasks of Chinese corporations that will operate along the BRI share only one commonality: high complexity.

Each project, from the Sino-Pakistani corridor (US$63 billion) to the Ogaden Basin Gas Pipeline in Ethiopia (US$5 billion) or the Mes Aynak copper mine in Afghanistan (US$3 billion), includes several layers of complexity ranging from financial, technical, operational, political and physical security risks, and greater complexity entitles greater risks.

The main risks related to the Chinese overseas interests, with the exception of the investments in financial structures (bonds, stocks, funds and futures), are summarized in three levels:

1. Liability (general, third party, employer's, environmental, etc.)
2. Construction—commercial
3. Political risk—terrorism—kidnap and ransom (K&R)—criminal risk

The third level is the one that is directly influencing how China needs to react in the employment of PSCs. While the energy sector has reached a certain degree of maturity in risk management and mitigation, the majority of the Chinese SOEs and private corporations that are interested in becoming active stakeholders along the BRI are still unaware of the complexity of the task. Several international security providers have underlined how the Chinese state energy companies are the only SOEs to have developed internal capabilities in risk assessment management and mitigation, due to previous 'unfortunate experiences'.[3] Since the beginning of the new century, it has been speculated that the number of attack on Chinese energy companies has been limited compared to Western counterparts, due to the fact that China's national energy companies are latecomers to the global market. An educated guess can be made regarding how secrecy, lack of transparency and the strategic role of Beijing's political infighting led to the shortage of open-source statistics on the SOEs' incidents. It is likely that Chinese energy sector SOEs have already learned how to cope with security risk the hard way.

A new driver in the market expansion of the Chinese private security sector is coming from the insurance sector. The Chinese insurance sector could become a real market 'invisible hand' in stimulating healthy competition in the growing Chinese private security sector. While the Chinese internal insurance market is booming in the mainland, the provision of external insurance services related to the Chinese FDI is still in its infancy. Moreover, the changes ignited by the BRI in the global economic system are going to increase the profits of the insurance service sector, resulting in an increase of available funds to PSCs. With the need to insure the timely deliverance of infrastructures along the BRI, the insurance sector loss avoidance drive will promote the employment of capable PSCs. Central government support of the fulfilment of the Chinese overseas interests, combined with the insurance sector's stimulus to secure the timely delivery of projects, will foster a better understanding in risk assessment, risk transfer and risk mitigation.

3.3 China's Overseas Interests

On 12 July 2016, South Sudan's Health Ministry said that at least 271 people were killed in Friday's clashes. The UN Security Council said in a press statement that the 15-nation UN body condemned in the strongest terms the escalation of fighting in Juba, and they expressed their sympathies and condolences to the families of Chinese peacekeepers who were killed or injured in the attacks (Xinhua 2016).

The artillery fire that ravaged Juba, the capital of South Sudan, hit an UN armoured vehicle and claimed the lives of two Chinese peacekeepers. In Sudan, Chinese investments in the oil sector amounts to 75% of foreign investment,[4] while South Sudan is looking for another US$1.9 billion in loans from the Chinese investment banks for key infrastructure investments.[5]

The increasing number of Chinese blue helmets along the areas in which the Chinese SOEs operate is a growing trend in Beijing's foreign footprint. Focusing on the Chinese overseas interests, one notices a profound shift in one of the key pillars in Chinese foreign policy: the principle of non-interference. The Chinese central government's security concerns abroad are summarized in the definition of Chinese overseas interests: maintenance of trade, protection of Chinese nationals and infrastructure overseas and, especially the security of mining, gas and oil supply routes, essential to China's economic transformation.

President Xi has intensified Chinese participation in peacekeeping operations. The change has not been limited to the volume of peacekeepers, but it has also included a shifting role played by Chinese blue helmets from non-combatant support (engineer and medical support) to armed infantry units. The number of UN Chinese peacekeepers in Sudan alone is 1000 units with combat capabilities, and is part of the broader People's Liberation Army (PLA) military's operation other than war (MOOTW) strategy (China Military.com 2017). While the volume of Chinese peacekeepers is surging, and the capabilities of the Chinese consular protection services are being upgraded, the number of incidents of violence towards Chinese citizens abroad, particularly in the African continent (China Daily 2016a), has also increased at a rapid pace.

China's overseas interests can be divided in the following categories:

- Construction projects contracting
- Access to natural resources
- Access to foreign technology
- Access to overseas market
- Financial investments vehicles

Chinese overseas contracting companies, particularly those involved in heavy industry and the construction, are first in line to gain from the new

Silk Road. While the Chinese economy has been slowing down towards a 'new normal', the most hard-hit sectors since 2011 are the ones that are now receiving a lifeblood transfusion with the BRI constructions contracts. Beijing's new plans for the BRI are not only going to fuel the recovery for the Chinese heavy industrial sectors, but are already increasing investor confidence in the overall construction sector, ranging from steel mills to concrete factories. After more than five years of falling commodity prices and an increasing level of industrial excess capacity,[6] confidence in the business has returned and the SOEs that are building along the BRI are starting to invest again. For the first time since 2011, there is an increase in heavy machinery sales due to international, government-led investments. As an example, the overall demand for excavators in China skyrocketed by 50% by the end of 2016 thanks to the BRI promises (Bloomberg 2016) of future contracts and gains. Unfortunately, up to the beginning of 2017 there was not much sign of interest in the overall SOEs' security apparatus upgrade.[7] SOEs' risk perception, as well as willingness to pay for international professional services, remains low, and the leading Chinese PSCs are still struggling to be considered as a service provider to the Chinese overseas interests.

Access to natural resources and the protection of logistical supply lines are also a fundamental part of the Chinese overseas interests, crucial to preserving strategic access to energy and the resources needed to sustain China's economic impulse.

In 1993, China became a net importer of hydrocarbons and energy security became a top priority for the central government. Chinese strategic planning in the energy sector is focused around three core pillars: strategic reserve accumulation, global access to multiple energy sources and increased efficiency in distribution and consumption.

In this respect, the choice of Central Asia as a natural resource supply base is part of Beijing's efforts to diversify its Middle East maritime supply (Blank 2006). The role of the BRI in Central Asia is of primary strategic importance for Beijing's national energy security. Starting with the gas pipeline in Turkmenistan, the Chinese energy SOEs have gradually broken the market monopoly owned by Russia in the region.[8] The choice of Turkmenistan is not by chance, as the country holds the world's largest reserve of natural gas. The overall cooperation is epitomized by the Chinese 1833 km natural gas pipeline that connects Turkmenistan with Xinjiang, through which will flow a projected annual supply of natural gas of 25 billion cubic metres. Also the number of Chinese energy M&A,

in the Central Asian region of the BRI, includes notable examples such as China National Petroleum's acquisition of 8% of the mining and drilling rights in the areas of Kashagan in Kazakhstan and other drilling rights in the Caspian Sea, worth respectively US$5 billion and US$3 billion. Beijing's subsequent activities in Kazakhstan include the cooperation between KazMunaiGaz and Sinopec (started in 2005) and the start of a series of takeovers that help China's energy SOEs acquire a strategically vital regional position. Another example is given by the takeover of PetroKazakhstan, a Canadian-registered company with all its assets located in Kazakhstan. The takeover guaranteed the full ownership of several Kazak oilfields not far from the China–Kazakhstan oil pipeline. All these areas require a security footprint that Chinese PSCs are competing to achieve. Local governments and security firms in the region are competing to partner with the Chinese PSCs in providing security service to Chinese workers and infrastructure. At the same time, Russian PSCs that share a language and military training with the Central Asian counterparts are starting to show interest in supporting Chinese security efforts.

As has happened in the African continent regarding Chinese mining operations, China's energy investments in Central Asia have repeatedly come under the spotlight due to negative impact on local communities, both environmentally and socially. Albeit the CSR policy awareness is promoted by the central government, there is still a widespread perception that Chinese companies are pursuing predatory policies, depleting local resources without any positive economic spillover into the local communities. In this respect, the lack of SOEs' CSR and the minimum investments in human resources talents by the Chinese PSCs represent a dangerous mix that could ignite violent confrontation with local workers and communities. Examples abound. In Kirgizstan, thousands of Chinese workers are employed in infrastructure projects and mines. Kyrgyz have grown suspicious that the Chinese could become the majority. The suspicion turned to hysteria, and riots followed shortly (Rikelton 2014). In Kazakhstan, International Crisis Group (ICG 2015) reports that 'workers in Aktobe have told Crisis Group that China's industrial presence in the oil rich region—including big influxes of Chinese workers—meant unfair pay, unsafe working conditions, and fewer job opportunities for Kazakhs. But misgivings cut both ways. A senior Chinese oil executive said he would rather work in Africa than Almaty because of the discrimination he and his family faced on a daily basis.'

In 2015 and 2016, the surge in Chinese ODI showcased a more confident China on the global scene.[9] Therefore, the increase of concerns and necessities over the China's overseas interests (COI) well emphasized how China's core national interests are increasingly linked with the expansion and security of the overseas ones. With Beijing's rising role as international investor, Chinese corporations in 2015 alone contracted US$61 billion in M&A, an increase of 14% from the previous year. While the overall Chinese outbound direct investments are still a fraction of the global M&A market, the first half of 2016 has witnessed the crossing of the US$100 billion threshold. Since his September 2015 speech at the United nations (UN) in New York[10] and G20 Summit in June 2016,[11] President Xi has underlined the risks in rising protectionism in global trade, with particular concern to the Chinese attempt to 'go global'. The Chinese leadership perceives protectionism as paramount risk to Chinese exports and the new wave of cross border M&A that Chinese companies have launched in the last few years.[12] As for political and financial risks associated with long-term regional infrastructural investments, unpredictability and uncertainty are Beijing's main concerns. At the same time, the perception of imminent security threats is gradually being acknowledged.

For the first time, China's 2015 military strategy white paper prioritized the role of Chinese overseas interests as one of the PLA's strategic tasks.

According to President Xi, who is also the chairman of the Central Military Commission, the Chinese army must change with the times into a smaller organization with greater combat capabilities and optimized structures.[13] During September 2015, under Xi's aegis, the PLA started restructuring and forcing optimization, with the demobilization of 15% of the 2.3 million personnel. According to the new Chinese scientific military principles, the downsizing process is still working towards smaller and better-optimized units, with an elite force at the core. Being the largest trading nation by the overall exchange of goods, the Chinese overseas interests represent the global reach that China has established over the last three decades since the opening up reforms carried by the leader Deng Xiaoping. Since joining the World Trade Organization (WTO) in 2001, China has increased threefold its share of exported goods, and Chinese mercantilism became a critical fixture of the world trading system. In 2009, China became the greatest exporter of goods, and in 2013 it became the biggest trading nation, with a total export of US$1.9 trillion

(Bloomberg 2013). After stumbling in the race with the United States to take first place as world's leading economy in 2015–2016, China's new wave of investments, spearheaded by the BRI, is poised to bridge the gap.

3.4 Global Interest Vs. Global Ambitions: Stretching the Non-interference Principle

> China today has two dilemmas: China doesn't harbor any global security ambition, but its interests are already global. (Zhou 2015)

Just after the bombing of the Chinese Embassy in the Kyrgyz capital of Bishkek, Foreign Ministry spokesperson Hua Chunying restated[14] how the safety of personnel abroad is of paramount importance, and that the Ministry of Foreign Affairs (MFA) is taking precautions to ensure the well-being of the Chinese personnel overseas. This first open blow to the BRI, although minor in itself, has urged Beijing to reconsider if the countries that host Chinese investments are able guarantee the safety of the Chinese nationals. Therefore, the creation of China's first military base abroad in Djibouti is the starting point of a broader military network to protect Chinese nationals overseas and to guarantee a steady flow of goods over the maritime Silk Road.

The city-state of Djibouti is the first milestone of China's global reach as a world power. In the past, Western[15] and Chinese analysts shared the view that Chinese investments in foreign commercial port facilities would allow China to expand its maritime power. A common perception was that Chinese investments in foreign civilian ports could lead to the development of forward military bases. Contrary to the predictions, the PLA's Navy (PLAN) choice to build from scratch the first Chinese military outpost abroad in Djibouti reveals China's firm resolve to protect its expanding overseas interests. Though paling in comparison to the 42 US military bases overseas, the tiny dot on the world map representing China's extension of its military reach into the Indian Ocean could cause concern in the near future. 'While Western nations have encouraged Chinese involvement in peacekeeping and other multilateral missions, a long-term military presence in Djibouti, butting up against US operations, opens a fresh arena of potential friction' (Page 2016).

Nevertheless, Djibouti represents a pivotal point in the Chinese attitude towards the four decades-old policy of non-intervention. Enunciated in 1953 by Prime Minister Zhou Enlai, the non-interference principle is one of the Five Principles of Peaceful Coexistence that constitute the pillars of the Chinese foreign policy.

However, the debate over the non-interference principle among Chinese and international academics is still open (Mathieu Duchatel 2014), and Beijing has already started to take a pragmatic and proactive stance in supporting its Core Overseas Interests. The non-interference principle was defined in a different international relations setting, when China was entangled in the long-standing trauma of the 'century of humiliation'.[16] However, the post–Cold War globalization process and China's rise as world power stretches the limit of non-interference. At the same time, Beijing's adherence to this decades-old principle still provides room for manoeuvre for China's soft power. Thus, while Beijing's posture in the East China Sea is challenging the view of China's 'peaceful rise', the principle is already being challenged in several areas ranging from Kyrgyzstan to Crimea. Moreover, some pre-eminent Chinese academicians have already started to question the validity of the principle proposing a Chinese 'constructive involvement' or a 'creative involvement'.[17] Many Chinese academicians still share a common view regarding the utility of non-interference in promoting China's overseas interests, projecting a non-hegemonic vision. Moreover, China has demonstrated on several occasions the ability to adapt the non-interference principle to its own advantage without squandering decades of adherence to the image of a socialist developing country. While increasing PLAN blue water capabilities (Erickson 2016), China has been following the central government guidelines in protecting Beijing's growing international interests. In practical terms, the employment of Chinese PSCs could affect the Chinese non-interference principle in both positive and negative ways.

The effects of the Chinese economic and political changes initiated in several countries that are involved in the BRI have demonstrated the necessity to adopt a multi-vector policy that balances US military power with the Chinese economic power. For example, Central Asian countries have reached a dynamic equilibrium between Russian security support and Chinese investments (Arduino 2015a). In the European landmass, Beijing's main concerns are related to Chinese market integration with the supply of natural resources. At the same time, Russia's integration of the former Soviet states in the Eurasian Economic Union openly competes with China. While Chinese integration is focused on the country's economic power, Russian integration is based on the country's military strength. The Eurasian countries' attitude towards China is less anxious than the attitude towards Russia. One of the reasons is that Moscow perceives Eurasia as a platform to guarantee a role as major power, while Beijing's 'peaceful rise' is still focused on economic power. That being said, the Chinese and Russian competing spheres of influence are balanced by Beijing's acceptance of Moscow's role in providing security.

> Economically-minded thinkers in Moscow criticize this arrangement for reducing Russia to a mere "security firm" guarding China's economic expansion. The Kremlin—which have a strong tradition of valuing hard power over soft and economic power—is not disturbed.[18]

Along with Central Asian international relations multi-vector policies, countries such as Djibouti are developing their own balancing strategies—in this case, hedging Chinese economic might against the United States' military primacy.

3.5 Securing the 'Chinese Dream': Narrowing the Gap Between Economic Diplomacy and Security Capabilities

The Chinese Dream of Rejuvenation of the country (Xin Hua 2016), which promoted an all-round moderately prosperous society by 2020, focuses on the continuation of positive economic momentum, anticipates a steady internal growth with an increase of gross domestic product (GDP) at an annual rate of 6.7%. China expects to maintain a stable growth rate and develop a domestic market capable of absorbing internal industrial overcapacity, and to transition to an economic model with higher value-added activities. The BRI has been implemented to achieve these ends, facilitating the Chinese economy's soft transition towards this new model. Contrary to assumptions made in 2001 when China entered the WTO, the new Chinese economic model is not led by economic liberalization, but by a state-led, top-down approach spearheaded by SOEs. The new SOEs are emerging from a consolidation period that began in the 1990s and was accelerated by the 2012 anti-corruption campaign. As a result, the surviving state' conglomerates have not only increased their commercial influence, but their political influence as well. In December 2012, when the 18th Party Congress inaugurated the fifth generation of Chinese leaders, President Xi Jinping first coined the phrase 'Chinese Dream', indicating the new direction of the party and, therefore, the country. While the idea behind the Chinese Dream is still lacking a detailed definition, the former key points of the 'harmonious society' and 'peaceful rise' are still part of a bigger picture, along with internal stability and wealth creation. In addition, China needs a stable international environment in order to secure supply chains and the market routes for its own exports. The 'Chinese Dream' policy presents an international call for stability and wealth creation. The Chinese leadership has stressed the importance of the role of BRI global connectivity in the 'Chinese Dream'. During November 2014, China's Beijing Asia Pacific Economic Cooperation (APEC) noted how free trade, better communications infrastructure and investment facilitation can develop a better sense of shared destinies (Xin Hua 2014).

Moreover, the 'Chinese Dream' and the related security issues developing along the BRI and in key areas, including Africa and Latin America, are a proving ground for the Chinese capability to ensure a 'Safe Dream'.

One example of Chinese economic diplomacy over the BRI occurred with the first failed Chinese bid to upgrade the Thai railway network. In 2013, Beijing and Bangkok announced the intention to develop two dual-track high-speed rail lines covering almost 900 km. The Thai parliament, following international pressure from competing bidders, voted down the proposal. Just one year later at the end of 2014, the same parliament approved the deal, presenting Chinese companies with the possibility to build the new rail network (China Daily 2016c) and to acquire an important share of Thai agricultural products and rubber exports.

While Chinese SOEs competing abroad have the full support of the Chinese banking system's economic diplomacy, the security sector must develop its own roots in Beijing's higher-level financial and political system. China does not have a military industrial complex (MIC) that can apply lobbying power on the government, such as in the United States. At the same time, the political reach of Russian MIC counterparts such as Rosoboronexport[19] still look more effective at influencing the Kremlin than Chinese companies such as Chinese Poly Technology or Norinco are at influencing Beijing.[20]

Since the Xi Jinping era began, China's economic diplomacy has been spearheaded by high-speed rail, energy and information and communications technology (ICT) connectivity (China Daily 2016b). However, security and risk assessment capabilities still lag behind, and the US$63 billion China-Pakistan Economic Corridor (CPEC) is the most telling example of this fact. CPEC includes a dangerous mix of volatile conditions that may be found all over the BRI. The Chinese bid to develop Pakistan's connectivity is riddled with technical, financial, security and political risks. Further, the timeline imposed on project delivery will not provide much of a learning experience pertaining to the localization of security needs. Unfortunately, Chinese business models based on 'crossing the river feeling the stones' do not fit the current security landscape. The market demand for force and the provision of efficient security services do not allow a second chance after a failure.

While China has already showcased resilience and capability in bidding and winning economic projects worldwide, there are still doubts over the positive spillover of these new macro projects. Chinese SOEs are accustomed to operating in a risk-free national environment where the main safety issues are related to hazardous working conditions, or the protests led by angry throngs of unpaid workers. Negative spillover examples in Mainland China include tragedies such as the Tianjin harbour explosion (Singapore Today 2015) and the Jiangxi power plant collapse (The Guardian 2016), which cost the lives of dozens of people. The international landscape, which is filled with political and criminal violence, presents a different setting to the Chinese SOEs that are used to operating in China with support granted by the central government.

International risk management practices are slowly entering the domain of Chinese SOEs, and privately run companies investing abroad. While some of the top Chinese players have reached the standards of Western counterparts, most of the other actors do not take into consideration geopolitical risks and related threats. The Chinese multinationals already showcasing risk mapping and scenario analysis capabilities belong to the energy, insurance and IT sector. This macro group of risk-aware companies well understand the value of how risk mapping enables the identification of present vulnerabilities and future threats. Chinese energy companies such as Sinopec possess in-house capabilities with a think tank devoted to analysing a broad spectrum of risks and cooperating with international security providers and other think tanks. Further, this macro group considers real-time monitoring of evolving political threats an important part of risk prevention, though widely recognized as a demanding exercise in terms of manpower. While the financial returns well outpace the costs of scenario analysis, only a small number of Chinese SOEs have this in-house capability. Most of the time it is outsourced to foreign specialists that support Chinese companies' ODI in spotting vulnerabilities related to political instability, terrorist threats and the spillover of Chinese investments onto local stakeholders. Managing geopolitical risk is not a new problem, but the pace imposed by new technologies made available by globalization tends to create ripple effects across the globe at high speed. Recent riots against the Chinese investment in Sri Lanka underscore how the new Chinese US$5 billion harbour project and the 15,000-acre industrial economic development zone will not only potentially create 100,000 new jobs but also provoke waves of angry protestors and discontents (The Economist 2017).

During SOE business meetings, imaginary lines have been traced over potential BRI trade routes, giving the perception of plentiful opportunities, yet estimating the economic viability of projects is a different problem. Localizing each project of the BRI to its own geographical and socio-political boundaries underlines how local risks, before and during the project development, are going to affect timing and cost assessment. As mentioned above, the main characteristic defining the overall BRI narrative is complexity.

The project's complexity is related not only to the specific local issues but also to the geopolitical concerns that arise in neighbouring countries, such as Russian discomfort over Chinese investment in Central Asia or Indian uneasiness over China's staggering economic support of Pakistan to the tune of US$63 billion. At the same time, threats to the realization of the BRI will catalyse a faster adoption of sophisticated risk management tools and stimulate the needed growth of the national PSCs with proven international capabilities. Chinese acceleration of outbound investments in infrastructure, logistic and ICT are already promoting a better integration of Chinese supply chains and easier access to international markets. Therefore, the integration of Chinese security providers into the broader market for force is just a matter of time. It remains to be seen if enlightened managers and policymakers are going to enable the development of mature PSCs, or if it is the blood toll paid in the coin of the lives of Chinese workers that will prompt the call for more sophisticated security services. The overall BRI narrative is linked to the efficiency of the new trade routes. The new logistic hubs are envisioned as lowering trade barriers, promoting access to Chinese capital for major infrastructure projects. While financial legal framework is developing at fast pace, it cannot be said for the security sector. Unfortunately, the BRI mainstream narrative discounts too easily local security concerns and overall geopolitical instability.

Further support in this direction could be promoted not only by the insurance sector, but also by the intervention of new financial institutions that China has capitalized on at the beginning of first decade of the new millennium, for example the Asia Infrastructure Investment Bank (AIIB; US$100 billion capital), the New Development Bank (also known as BRICS Bank US$100 billion capital) and the New Silk Road Financial Foundation (US$40 billion capital). These institutions, led by China, are posed to play a significant role in shifting international governance on trade sharing, as well as security issues at a multilateral level. Since joining the WTO in 2001, China's state-centred approach to international trade has witnessed a conceptual leap from rule-taker to rule-maker. While the Chinese preferential approach to security has been government-to-government (G2G) relations, intervention by new financial institutions could ignite a multilateral approach involving several states in the definition and provision of private security services.

Since 2000, China has gradually adapted to Western-dominated multilateral institutions, such as the International Monetary Fund (IMF) and the UN. A decade later, Beijing started to develop and steadily institutionalize in the international context its own institutions. These new alternatives are related to trade and finance, but it is not unfounded to forecast an increasing role of non-exclusively financial multilateral institutions such as the Shanghai Cooperation Organization (SCO) in which China holds more influence. One of the first steps in this direction is China requesting the SCO club for intensified intelligence sharing and for the organization members to track and prevent Chinese citizens from moving to jihadist-controlled areas for military training (Yang 2016).

Multilateral investments with international companies could dilute the Chinese SOEs' short- and medium-term risks, especially in the security arena. Nevertheless, the BRI is still deeply rooted in G2G partnerships. Beijing's preferred choice is to minimize the role of foreign intervention only to specific areas that Chinese corporations are not yet able to cover. Despite the promise of a more market-oriented approach, the prominence of governmental top-down policymaking based on the five-year economic plan is apparent, and Beijing continues to support SOEs. Instead of promoting the long-awaited market liberalization and related SOE reforms, Beijing is dictating how the market has to move.

BRI openness to foreign participation will determine how the local population receives both Chinese investments and an influx of Chinese migrant workers. The overall resentment towards Chinese companies in several areas of the globe contains a mixture of negative spillovers generated by the SOEs and a lack of CSR standard practices.

Additionally, rising Chinese protectionism, whether real or perceived, will increase threats of violence and insecurity for Chinese labour abroad. An example of intertwined global political problems and local grievances against Chinese investments is seen in anti-Chinese protests that occurred in Vietnam in May 2014. Vietnam is still considered by Chinese investors to be a favourable place to relocate production plants, as Vietnamese industrial parks offer competitive labour wages in a low-risk and stable socio-economic environment. On 11 May 2014, thousands of peaceful demonstrators rallied in major Vietnamese cities against China's installation of an oilrig in disputed waters claimed by Vietnam. On May 14, several riots erupted in the Vietnamese industrial zone of Binh Duong province where dozens of Chinese factories were looted and burned to the ground (Eva Dou 2014). Although the initial spark for the protests was a political claim in the contested South China Sea, the rise of uncontrolled violence has been linked to grievances against working conditions in Chinese factories. China's prompt reaction facilitated the evacuation of more than 3000 Chinese workers while several were reported dead and hundreds injured in the riots.

According to the BRI Big Data Report (2016), a collection of 300 billion pieces of information clustered and analysed by the State Information Center, Russia and Kazakhstan (Wang 2016) ranked as first and second respectively in a list of 64 countries' performance in cooperation with China's BRI. The report analysed how China and the 64 countries along the BRI cooperated over five key areas, including policy communication, connectivity, trade, finance and public support. According to the report, the following countries were China's top partners: Thailand, Pakistan and Indonesia. The report also underlines how in the lower end of the 32 ranked countries there is still a necessity to address better communication and procedures on the Chinese side. Beside the numbers on the size of Chinese outbound investments and related statistics, one data point is missing: the level of security dedicated to each investment. Prof Zhai Kun from Peking University addresses this problem, suggesting that 'the annual report should focus more on strategic indexes, such contribution degree of joint development' (Wang 2016). Nevertheless, a clear vision of each security need has to be indexed and evaluated for each infrastructure project, and global spillover produced from said projects must be calculated. Even in this broader research approach to the BRI, the security element is still missing from Beijing's strategic mapping.

3.6 Sino-Pakistan 'All Weather Friendship'

In China's modern history, several China watchers have defined the Chinese strategic partnership with other countries as a temporary setting that is going to change as fast as the sands of geopolitical equilibrium. Therefore, one is surprised to see the Sino-Pakistan 'all weather friendship' (Kabraji 2012) counting US$63 billion in planned investments. When it comes to Chinese ODI, it is always necessary to differentiate from pledged investment and actual realized investment, as seen in Africa during the 1990s. Most of the time, the stated numbers do not equal the realized investments, or are just the sum of previous and ongoing ODI. But in the case of CPEC, even if the sum of US$63 billion is not fully reached, it is undoubtedly one of the largest Chinese investment projects abroad. The CPEC is at the core of the BRI initiative, not only in absolute financial but also in geopolitical terms. The CPEC comprises China's western Xinjiang province region, populated predominantly by ethnic Muslims, and volatile security situations exist along the belt in several Pakistani regions that are riddled with ethnic conflict, terrorist threats and interregional disputes. Also, several areas along the CPEC that are supposed to benefit from Chinese investments could witness the sudden disappearance of Chinese funds. A shift in Chinese investment towards the more developed provinces such as Punjab, due to better political lobbying in Islamabad, could ignite anti-Chinese resentment in areas not poised to benefit from sudden influx of Yuan.

The economic corridors are a substantial part of the Chinese bid to revive trade across Central Asia into Europe via railways, ports and highways. According to the initial CPEC blueprints, US$11 billion will be allocated exclusively to connectivity and energy infrastructure. Since 2011, with the gradual erosion of US-Pakistan security and economic cooperation, the Sino-Pakistani friendship has progressively strengthened. Though rhetoric is espoused by the two countries about an 'all weather friendship', the cooperation is not based on common cultural or ideological values, but pragmatic economic and security necessities. These necessities range from the common fight against terrorism to balancing Indian-US relations in the area.

Since 2010, a nefarious mix of internal frictions and tensions with neighbouring countries has resulted in increased levels of Pakistani political violence.

Examples can be drawn on daily basis, ranging from improvised explosive device (IED) attacks to assaults on police stations and religious structures. In 2016 alone, the military campaign military against the Pakistani Taliban, as well as the Sunni-Muslim Lashkar-e-Jhangvi, triggered a backslash of terrorist bombing in the Baluchistan provincial city of Quetta, killing more than 70 people.[21] The independent incidents in Baluchistan, however, did not generate great concern as they were a localized threat compared to the international risks posed by terror organizations operating along the Pakistani borders, such us the Taliban and Islamic State (IS). Unfortunately, one of the three Chinese economic corridors will cross through all of Baluchistan. Baluchistan will be a key strategic area, hosting infrastructure and facilitating passage of Chinese goods from the northern Pakistan border region with China, flowing to the Indian Ocean port city of Gwadar in the province's southwest. The CPEC blueprint for the Chinese-funded Pakistani port city of Gwadar is intended to significantly reduce travel time between China and the Middle East. China is focused on securing a route to the Indian Ocean that would reduce dependence on the choke point of the Strait of Malacca between the Malay Peninsula and the Indonesian island of Sumatra. The Gwadar deepwater port is one of the key strategic segments of the CPEC, linking shipments of Chinese goods between the Arabian Sea and western China. Furthermore, with the opening of the Iranian economy and increase in oil exports, the Gwadar connection will provide a safer route for Chinese energy imports. The other Western economic corridor is influenced not only by Pakistani internal tensions but also by the rise in strife on the India-Pakistan border. In 2016 alone, the disputed area of Kashmir between India and Pakistan witnessed several exchanges of artillery shelling.

During the second week of November 2015, the first large shipment of Chinese goods from the city of Kashgar that passed through the unstable Chinese Xinjiang Uygur autonomous region arrived in Gwadar by road, indicating the trade route will be built there in the next two years. As said by Chinese Ambassador to Pakistan, Sun Weidong, 'It proves the connectivity of local roads, and realization of the concept of one corridor with multiple passage' (China Daily 2016b). Pakistan's prime minister Nawaz Sharif witnessed the first arrival of Chinese shipments to Gwadar, underlining how the strategic position of Pakistan and Chinese infrastructure projects will benefit a great area, and promote the integration of China, Central Asia and South Asia (China Daily 2016b-Ibidem).

According to the Pakistan's planning, development and reform minister Ahsan Iqbal, more than three quarters of the pledged US$63 billion will be implemented in 2017. At the end of 2016, however, the slow progress in the development of the CPEC has challenged the entire idea of the BRI. The staggering pledge to finance US$63 billion in infrastructure projects has put the CPEC at the forefront of the BRI, and any demise of the planned projects may entirely undermine confidence in the global initiative.

The first confidence-building measure from Islamabad comes in the form of a 15,000-strong, army-led security force deployed to protect Chinese personnel working along the corridor.[22] The economic corridors are riddled with complications, due to the impressive amount of funds pledged to the CPEC and to the unfortunate security and political circumstances seen in several Pakistani provinces. The role of Chinese PSCs as well as international PSCs that previously operated in the area is complicated by legal constraints in providing private armed services. At the same time, the military–civil government competition on the control of the security budgets and the cash flow derived by CPEC is another cause of concern for Beijing.

Considering the risks posed to the BRI in certain unstable regions of Pakistan, as well as the potential scope of the BRI's economic and security footprint in the area, further review of medium- and long-term investments is urgent.

Pakistani security challenges could be mitigated through several components, starting with the financial vehicles that will support the projects. Chinese foreign currency reserves are still capable of sustaining the initial thrust of the BRI, but further financial support must be found in the market through debt and in equity financial investments, as China is not going to pay all the bills indefinitely. International stakeholders already present in the AIIB or the SRF could provide the new financial vehicles, but the investment sustainability is related to predicted value creation for stakeholders. Unfortunately, incidents, delays, terrorist attacks or local political unwillingness to cooperate with the Chinese SOEs, as well as uncontrollable phenomena such as natural disasters, all tend to discourage private participation.

With the Chinese 'New Normal'[23] economic model aimed at a stable GDP increase of 6.5% per year, it will not be easy for the People's Bank of China to freely use further foreign reserves in order to support the BRI.

Like financial complications, security measures also need to be viewed in the long term. Beijing is in a hurry to deploy basic security measures and begin construction, whereas competing Pakistani ministries are still in the process of deciding respective leadership roles and interests.

Besides potential repercussions stemming from the CPEC's financial sustainability, or lack thereof, the infrastructure network involves provincial areas far from Islamabad's control that are marked by widespread instability, internal security problems and limited administrative capabilities. While Beijing attaches great importance to cooperation with neighbouring states, the 'all weather friendship' with Islamabad is not going to guarantee the same relationship at the provincial level.

One sign of impatience from the Chinese side is the rush to include the Pakistani military in the security design of the overall investment proposal. Several problems arise from the fact that the army is also interested in the leadership of the overall corridor projects. Throughout Pakistan's history, civilian-military relations have always been fragile and in constant flux. The Pakistani government is also facing pressure from different ministries competing for control of Chinese projects. At the same time, the Pakistani army bid is not totally unreasonable, as the army already possesses in-house capability to provide engineers and infrastructural project expertise.[24] Therefore, the active involvement of the Pakistan Army may provide Beijing with an improved sense of security. At the same time, since the year 2016 Beijing has become one of Pakistan's main defence suppliers (Price 2011). Unlike Western countries, China is not prone to impose export sanctions on Pakistan for defence equipment, and the level of high-tech exchange can be seen in the selling of China's JF 17 aircraft to Pakistan, as well as joint military exercises between the state's armies. Further, as part of the Central Asian anti-terrorist campaign, China has begun supplying counter-terrorism equipment to neighbouring countries including Pakistan.

Moreover, the influx of Chinese Yuan is already generating a hiatus in the country's civil-military relationship. The divide between the army and the government will be exacerbated at the local level where the resource allocation will be scarcer. Therefore, licensing of Chinese PSCs allied to the military or local police will be subject not only to the rule of law, but also to political power games among competing forces.

In terms of local and international PSCs, Pakistan offers a wide array of domestic solutions that present in main cities from Islamabad to Karachi. The list provided includes international companies such as G4S with offices both in the capital and in Karachi, and local ones such as Haris Enterprise security, Phoenix Security, Zims Securities, Security 2000 and Wackenhut Pakistan Pvt Ltd.

A first timid step taken by Chinese PSCs in the area is cooperation with local PSCs, with Chinese personnel acting as security managers inside Chinese workers' compounds while the Pakistani army and foreign PSCs work on the outside. The severity of the threats to Chinese nationals, and the complexity of the risk map over all Pakistan will be a difficult benchmark for all the Chinese PSCs involved in the project's security. At the same time, failures and international best practice are going to serve as a testing ground for the adoption of more efficient security models all around the BRI.

3.7 Central Asia Energy and Security Network

Central Asia's convoluted socio-economic and political transitions have generated a complex web of security threats and risks. Within the region, the level of political stability varies. While the Kazakhstan, Turkmenistan and Uzbekistan regimes' stability can rely on the profusion of natural resources and foreign investment, Tajikistan and Kyrgyzstan struggle for economic and socio-political stability. Since 2008 the economic relations between China and the five Central Asian republics have gradually expanded beyond trade to include a broad range of cooperation projects. Beijing's investment in the region increased at an unprecedented rate compared to several other BRI partners. The Chinese investment pattern in the region is similar to the one implemented over all the BRI: preferential loans directly managed by the MOFCOM and state-owned investment banks such as the China Development Bank and the Export-Import Bank of China (Arduino 2017). The Chinese economic synergy with the young Central Asian republics is focused on oil, gas and mining exports to China with a counterflow of Chinese FDI and consumer goods.

Since 2013 the BRI's scope in Central Asia has been diversified from the energy and mining sectors to infrastructural investments, with additional key logistical projects. Therefore, the road network upgrading and the high-speed railways are developed in order to enhance connectivity between China's Xinjiang autonomous region and the neighbouring Central Asian countries. The new Kyrgyz highway and the upgrade of the Uzbek rail network are just, perhaps, portion of the contracts that Chinese SOEs have started in the region. More ambitious logistical projects are related to the expansion of railway lines like those in Uzbekistan, Pakistan and Afghanistan. The overall BRI projects in the region are expected to enhance market integration with China, albeit Central Asian regional integration is still a long way away from fruition due to geopolitical concerns.

Besides the last decade of increasing economic cooperation and trade links between China and the young Central Asian republics, several security threats are going to influence the Chinese BRI. The hazards in the region range from local politics and internal struggles for power to historical stigma against Chinese influence. Despite the official BRI rhetoric emphasizing cooperation, China faces evident distrust from local populations. While the locals mostly welcome the influx of the Yuan, there is a diffuse resentment and fear over Chinese migrant workers. Since the time of the tsars in the nineteenth century, propaganda machines have stimulated a perception of population imbalance between locals and Chinese migrants (Lim 2013) that were prone to settle in the region. Although recent fieldwork based data (Portyakov 2006) from Russia's Far East do not support the prediction that Chinese workers are there to stay, after more than a century the imagined conception of a population imbalance has taken roots in the region.

The overall BRI footprint has already resulted in serious incidents due to a lack of CSRs, as well as the absence of policies devoted to avoiding environmental degradation, work-related accidents and corruption. These kinds of accidents had ignited tensions and caused confrontation between Chinese workers and local populaces.

At the same time, the political risks associated with regime instability cast a shadow over the prospects of BRI long-term return on investment. While the Turkmen and the Uzbek succession of power after the death of both 'fathers of the nation' have not led to forecast social instability, it is still too early to discount any threat from the succession of Kazakhstan's ageing leader. Besides the opaque leadership succession policy, renewed outbreaks of Islamic separatism and the distrust over Chinese presence are a clear and present danger to transnational integration.

China's interaction with the Central Asian countries is closely linked with energy, politics and security. A pre-eminent example is the Turkmenistan–China natural gas pipeline, which not only ensures a steady flow of natural gas to the Xinjiang autonomous province but also displays the Turkmen government's choice of the Chinese SOE Sinopec over the former Russia Gazprom. The growth of Chinese influence in Central Asia can be seen as a by-product of the changing power balance between Beijing and Moscow since the end of the Cold War (Eder 2014). While in the geopolitical arena China and Russia have found common ground in counterbalancing US influence, in Central Asia the competition is open.[25] At the same time, Moscow's firm grip on regional security is not a guarantee for the protection of the Chinese investments as was the case in Iraq and Afghanistan during the US military interventions.

While China and Russia compete for regional economic development, they find a common path in military cooperation that resists the 'three evils' of extremism, separatism and terrorism.[26] South and Central Asia's socio-political instability is going to affect not only China's western borders but also the Eurasian land bridge section of the BRI. Additionally Beijing faces the threat of internal fragility of the Kyrgyzstan and Tajikistan regimes and the unpredictability linked with the succession of ageing founding leader in Kazakhstan.[27] Ripple effects from a crisis could have devastating consequences, and one must consider the risks posed by the outbreak of riots in the Xinjiang autonomous province. On this point it is possible to infer an increase in the trafficking of heroin, weapons and money laundering. However, the predicted flow of veteran jihadists, returning to their territories of origin, has yet to be seen. Since 2014, the attacks claimed by ETIM near the city of Kashgar (Xinhua 2013) and the border areas of Xinjiang have increased in terms of quantity, but there has been no escalation in terms of weapon or tactical sophistication that would announce the beginning of a new phase of terror. Besides the fact that the status of military cooperation between Central Asia and China is linked with the SCO framework of multilateral cooperation, the last decade has witnessed a growing engagement of PLA and People's Armed Police (PAP) in joint bilateral military exercises and training programmes over the SCO's borders. In particular, bilateral exercises and information sharing between China and the individual SCO countries has increased compared to the utilization of the multilateral Regional Anti-terrorist Structure (RATS) based in Tashkent.[28] Therefore, China's leading economic footprint in Central Asia is going to force Beijing to enact security and political actions in the region (Arduino 2017). While the G2G and SCO multilateral cooperation takes place, the privatization of the market for force in Central Asia is involving not only the local actors interested in a share of the market, but also Russian PSCs that have a good knowledge of the post-Soviet regions and the advantage of using the Russian language.

3.8 Afghanistan's Great Game

Since the 2014 partial withdrawal of US and International Security Assistance Force (ISAF) collation forces from Afghanistan, Pakistan has become an important ally for China in formulating new policies for regional stability. In geopolitical terms, Afghanistan is the linchpin between Central Asia and South Asia. Therefore, the Afghan nexus involves China and Central Asia but also the core interests of several regional powers including India, Pakistan, Iran, and Turkey. China's economic diplomacy, more than the active involvement of the PLA, could be the nexus between Afghanistan's stabilization and regional economic integration with Central Asia (Arduino 2015b). The China-led commitment to building the BRI logistic and economic infrastructures and trade integration in South and Central Asia could begin an effective stabilization process. In this respect, Afghanistan links the BRI's North-South axis transit lines influencing the Eurasian land bridge. While Chinese investments in military modernization will enable Beijing in the mid- to long term to increase the PLA's scope and range, in the short term, China's chief instrument to influence regional outcomes still involves economic tools (Arduino 2015a) and a proactive stance in the employment of PSCs.

Year 2015 marked the 60th anniversary of bilateral diplomatic relations between China and Afghanistan. In the BRI blueprint, Afghanistan not only represents a neighbouring country, but also is a key actor in several economic projects. Furthermore, both China and Russia are concerned that a rapid deterioration of Kabul's grip over the country's security will destabilize South and Central Asia, increasing the chances of Islamic extremism. Increased instability around Kabul casts a wider shadow over the local Chinese direct investment, forcing Beijing to slow down future initiatives. However, the sudden collapse of Kabul's government is posed to create even greater damage to China's BRI larger economic footprint in Central Asia and on its own western borders. During the 15th SCO[29] summit held in Russia, Chinese president Xi Jinping met his Afghan counterpart Ghani on the side, pledging to increase security cooperation between the two countries and to provide security equipment and training to the Afghan National Army (ANA) (Xin Hua 2015). Furthermore, Russian president Vladimir Putin underlined the risks of the expansion of

Islamic militant groups in the region, and has assured to reinforce the Russian border patrol division deployed in Tajikistan.[30] Although Moscow's assertive foreign policy in Syria has been showcasing Russia's renewed military capabilities, with precision air strikes and long-range cruise missiles, it is not viable to predict an engagement in the area as similar as the 1979–1989 Soviet-Afghan war, as this remains an open wound.

There has been an overall slowdown in previous Chinese outbound direct investments in Afghanistan, ranging from the symbolic Mes Aynak[31] copper mine near Kabul to more ambitious infrastructure projects that include a railway connection with Pakistan. Quoting the Chinese vice minister of commerce Gao Yan:

> At present, the "Belt and Road Initiative" proposed by Chinese President Xi Jinping has entered into the implementation stage. Afghanistan is an important country along the line of the Silk Road Economic Belt. China praises that Afghanistan positively responds and participates in the construction of the Silk Road Economic Belt and China will work with Afghanistan as well as other countries along the line to give full play to the comparative advantages of each other, promote the docking of the development strategy, improve the level of trade and economic cooperation and realize a mutual beneficial and common development.[32]

On the diplomatic side, China is actively involved in trilateral talks with their Pakistani and Afghanistan counterparts as well as with the Afghan government's dialogue with the Taliban. Chinese anxiety stems more from the threat of radicalization spreading across Central Asia than with the Afghan Taliban itself. In December 2014 and May 2015, Beijing diplomats have actively promoted direct talks between representatives of the Afghan government and the Afghan Taliban. In February 2015, China endorsed a high-level dialogue between Afghanistan and Pakistan's foreign affairs ministers, assuring the financial and technical expertise in several cooperation projects ranging from a railway connection from Islamabad to Kabul to a hydroelectric plant to produce energy for both countries. At the same time, the confirmed death of the Taliban leader Mullah Omar stalled the negotiation, while the increasing presence of IS militants in the region has added further instability. Nevertheless, China's move towards the role of mediator represents a foreign policy shift. Beijing is already aware that China's active involvement in the Afghan affair will generate new vulnerabilities. However, Chinese diplomacy still has many a card to play, due to the low profile Beijing has long played in the region. China denied the United States access to its own territory for transit of military convoys during the ISAF pacification efforts, which fostered a perception amongst the Afghan population that China was neutral.

> Whether China can succeed in an area where so many have failed is questionable. Chinese diplomats do have the advantage of representing a growing regional power with enormous economic assets that enjoys a rare neutral image in Afghanistan. As noted, Beijing has not sent its troops to the country and its security assistance has been low key. (Weits 2015)

Nevertheless, Chinese diplomatic efforts are increasing related to finding a possible solution to contain the fall of Kabul. During trilateral talks in Moscow, China, Russia and Pakistan warned of increased IS influence in Afghanistan (Hobson 2016). The progressive deterioration of Kabul's control over the country has led the three states to progressively open to the Taliban.

Afghanistan, along with several other states, has acquired Chinese technology and infrastructure in exchange for the granting of natural resources to Chinese SOEs—these companies will have to go to great lengths to protect Chinese interests and personnel. Several Chinese PSCs currently provide security services to Chinese oil and mining companies near Kabul (Arduino 2015c), but the private security condition is in dire need of an upgrade. The surge in the provision of private security services faces several obstacles, ranging from the new laws against private armed security services, to the tarnished image left in the minds of countrymen by international contractors on the US payroll.

The Afghan problems related to the handling of PSC duties and obligations offer interesting case studies for Chinese strategists and lawmakers. Afghan cases of mismanagement, mistakes and corruption as well as daily security threats to the workers' lives showcased how billion-dollar projects in unsafe areas require qualified men with significant power in order to ensure the safety of the workers and the realization of projects. Just throwing money at the problem is not a viable long-term solution. In the recent past, both misuse of funds to contract Afghan warlord militias and unaccountable international PSCs have further deteriorated an already-critical situation. A clear example can be seen in August 2010, when President Hamid Karzai issued a personal decree against the use of PSCs. The decree forced international PSCs to exit the country by

December 2010. The decree showed how Karzai, former employer of international PSCs such as Blackwater for his personal protection, deemed unwelcome external security providers in order to avoid 'horrific and tragic incidents' (Reuters 2010).

At the same time, the decree well underlines the poisonous negative spillovers that unaccountable PSCs could ignite in the delicate local equilibrium. Abusive and ineffective actions seen perpetrated by PSCs in Afghanistan can be used as a guideline in today's volatile world, preventing history from repeating itself. During the Karzai presidency, 52 registered PSCs employed at least 30,000 contractors.[33]

The main problems related to the PSC footprint in Afghanistan are summarized by:

- Employment of local tribal militias that could use their PSCs status to perpetrate local feuds or extort money at gunpoint
- Illegal trade, acquisition and stockpiling of weapons that could fall into insurgents' hands
- Leaking of classified information compromising the army's effort
- Hindrance of efforts to conquer the local population's hearts and minds
- Attracting local talents, undermining the government efforts to strengthen the national government and security force
- Promoting corruption, including paying bribes to insurgents to avoid attacks
- Creating parallel security structures

At the same time, the General Stanley McChrystal of the US Army, who under the Obama presidency threw his support behind the ban, vented over how the coalition in Afghanistan became too dependent on private contractors (Hastings 2010). Nevertheless, the reality of the terrorist and criminal violence embedded in the country has forced a slower implementation of the PSC ban, as not only the US Army but also diplomatic personnel, NGOs and the press are unable to find suitable a replacement for their protection.

China has long been concerned that instability in Afghanistan will spill over into violence-prone Xinjiang and affect investments in Pakistan. China's military presence in Afghanistan is a matter of speculation since 2015. Since the retreat of the US-led coalition in Afghanistan, China appeared to promote a deeper Russian and Pakistani involvement in Kabul's affairs.

> For Beijing, a stable and secure Afghanistan is both key to domestic security as well as its growing investments in Pakistan. (Pantucci 2017)

At the same time, Beijing's growth as regional security actor is increasing India's suspicions over Chinese support to Islamabad. In this respect China employs a wide array of tools ranging from the multilateral organization such as the SCO, the Conference on Interaction and Confidence-Building Measures in Asia (CICA) and 'Istanbul Process' to the Quadrilateral Cooperation and Coordination Mechanism (Afghanistan, China, Pakistan, Tajikistan). The increased call for Chinese PSCs in Kabul is an additional tool to Beijing international projection arsenal. The Chinese security role is confirmed by the visit of leading military officials in Kabul as well as the inclusion of Afghanistan in the Belt initiative with promises of substantial infrastructural investments. In November 2016, Assistant Foreign Minister Kong Xuanyou underlined during his officials meeting in Kabul the development of future railway links between Quetta, Peshawar and Kabul. In March 2016, China's military chief of staff Fang Fenghui's visit to Kabul confirmed Beijing's direct involvement in Afghanistan's security problems. Furthermore, Mr Prince's involvement in the establishment of a training camp for private security personnel in the neighbouring Xinjiang province is a further step in this direction. Xinjiang shares a 50 km border with Afghanistan but the impervious mountain conditions do not facilitate any kind of transit. In this respect, the PLA footprint in the area is more oriented to improve the Tajikistan border control capabilities avoiding a possible rout for Uighur fighters returning in Xinjiang after their Afghan training.

All the aforementioned negative effects could hinder Chinese economic-led stabilization and endanger Chinese corporation's personnel operating in the area. The Chinese SOEs' and PSCs' future role in Afghanistan is not only affected by the highly unstable political context but also by the evolution of the Afghan ban and laws that constrict the scope and employment of foreign PSCs. New regulations enacted after the formal ban on international, private armed activity previously carried on by international PSCs force foreign clients to engage local PSCs. Specific to the Afghan context, Chinese SOEs have to rely on several layers of protection guarantees, ranging from local tribal militia up to the ANA. At the same time, the safety of the Chinese diplomatic personnel is guaranteed by the PLA. That being said, the new framework of laws still allows some space for Chinese PSCs to be employed, acting as a bridge between local security forces and Chinese enterprise. This enterprise is in need of crisis management, security planning and basic training for personnel due to be sent to work in dangerous areas.

3.9 Africa: From Libya to Sudan

> Against the backdrop of heightened risk from kidnapping, piracy, insurgent attacks, banditry, and other threats, the security business in Africa is booming. Predominantly ex-servicemen of U.S., European, and Israeli descent lead more than 80% of these security firms. As the market opens up, and more and more Chinese SOEs see the need for protection, it seems Chinese contractors are also increasingly aiming to expand overseas. (Lee 2014)

China's love story with Africa stems from a long-standing relationship that dates back to the 1970s, but since the new millennium, it has been said 'the honeymoon' is over'.[34]

The BRI's renewed thrust in promoting Chinese outbound investments in Africa is repackaging the old Chinese policies of supporting the African nations while absorbing the natural resources outputs and modernizing local infrastructure with updated Chinese ones. Renewed ties in key BRI areas such as Ethiopia and Djibouti will lead to benefits from the new cooperation, infrastructure and business investments (China Daily 2016a). At the same time, the new African BRI narrative is riddled by old problems stemming from the Chinese economic footprint in the continent.

Since the 1970s, Chinese corporations operating in the African continent have witnessed several security risks that threatened investments and Chinese workers abroad. Compared to today's security landscape, the main differences are related not to the severity of the threat, but to the perception that risks are going to affect the narrative of the BRI, and the growing doubts of the Chinese population towards Beijing security capabilities in protecting Chinese nationals abroad.

While China is not completely detached from the narrative of sustaining Third World countries, the new economic embrace of the continent has begun increasing Beijing's security responsibilities in the area, a role it has been 'unwilling' to take thus far.

The international PSC legacy in the African continent includes a lasting, negative memory of abuse, with the term 'mercenary' riddled with negative connotations. Mercenary groups like the German Landsknecht were synonymous with brutality and disease during the Italian peninsular conflicts of the fifteenth century, and the role played by foreign mercenaries in Africa since the 1970s has only cemented this kind of attitude towards groups like modern PSCs. Since the 1970s, infamous atrocities perpetrated by adventurers like leader of the French 'les affreux' (Keaten 2007) have been linked to all private military corporations that have perpetuated insecurity across the continent.

Nowadays, most African states are unable to cope with internal instability and external threats. Power vacuums and weak governments still attract the employment of private contractors in order to guarantee state or multinationals' security and ensure a monopoly over the continent's abundant mining resources. Even the UN is employing PSCs, considering them a necessary evil. The current UN framework of regulation against the employment of mercenaries is an open condemnation of violence and disregard human rights perpetrated by mercenaries during Africa's postcolonial wars.

Nevertheless, UN peacekeeping missions in several states, from Sierra Leone to Ethiopia, have resorted to a necessary evil: PSCs. These services contracted by UN missions range from close protection of the UN staff to humanitarian convoy armed escort, as well as specialized programmes such as mine clearance. Again, the debate on the role of PSCs ranges between two extremes. The first is related to the presumption of efficiency of the private sector compared to the weak African governments incapable of maintaining a monopoly of force. The second considers PSCs as simply pursing war profiteering, thus nothing more than a business prone to abuse that commits crimes against humanity perpetrated by unaccountable soldiers of fortune.

Recently, a commonly shared perception is that use of PSCs is not compatible with solving conflicts in Africa, and in some cases, the usage has contributed to a perpetual state of insecurity. PSCs are commonly accused of being unable to support the state's ability to retain a monopoly on the use of force. Additionally, examples from the recent past showcase where PSCs facilitated continued insecurity for the sake of profit. (See: The failed coup in Sierra Leone promoted by Sandline [Singer 2007].)

Recent example of Libya and the regional power vacuum generated by the demise of the historical dictator Muhammad Gaddafi showcases the employment of mercenaries from local sub-Saharan states or former Soviet bloc countries.

During the peak of the Gaddafi regime, most of the airplane and helicopter pilots, as well as mechanics and technical specialists for the maintenance of sophisticated weapons platforms, were from Ukraine. When the wind of revolution that blew during the Arab Spring ignited protest in the streets of Benghazi in February 2011, Gaddafi employed several units of Chadian and Nigerian mercenaries as well as untrained and undisciplined sub-Saharan workers to quell the demonstrations. The black African workers entitled to the use of force by the state were recognized not only by the different colour of their skin but also by the yellow worker's helmets they wore while attacking the population. Along with foreign African mercenaries, several Russian and Serbian snipers also engaged in fire support during the last defence of Gaddafi's stronghold in the country's capital, Tripoli.

As it is still the case in other African and Middle Eastern countries, the loyal support of mercenaries is perceived as essential against internal attacks. Mercenary units do not have tribal affiliation, and their ethnic traits, language differences and, crucially, salaries guarantee their temporary loyalty. In the case of Gaddafi, the preferred choice of mercenary came from the Tuareg tribes. The Tuareg nomadic heritage made them outsiders in the Libyan power game, and their culture resembled the Bedouin tribe to which Gaddafi belonged.

When the Benghazi uprising developed into a full-scale insurgency, Gaddafi's desperate bid to retain power was focused on the employment of a wide array of mercenaries along the thinning lines of regime loyalists. As soon as the tide of the civil war started to turn in favour of the rebels, mercenaries tried to flee the country. Several hundred were imprisoned and summarily executed. The lack of loyalty and side-switching that was noted as soon as the situation deteriorated against the government is one of the main differences between an armed fanatic and an armed contractor. The latter is going to reach a point where there is no price that will hold him in the fight once the winning momentum is gone. Mercenaries deserting when the end of their master is near, or changing sides during the conflict, is not news. The Chinese Song dynasty historians underlined how a warlord's armies are absorbed into their ranks as defeated armies. Machiavelli's The Prince warns against the employment of free lancers. The Libyan case as well as the last three decades on the African continental history is testament to the case.

Another forewarning comes from Libya, where the coastal city of Benghazi provides another contemporary historical example highlighting the negative effects of PSC usage. On 11 September 2012, heavily armed militants stormed the US diplomatic outpost in the city, overrunning international and local PSCs. The local militia deployed to defend the American diplomats fled before engaging the attackers, and the promised Libyan interim government military support arrived well after the attack had ended. The mostly unknown British PSC Blue Mountain Group (Reuters 2017) and local personnel were not able to protect ambassador Christopher Stephens, besieged in Benghazi's US diplomatic compound. The death of the ambassador along with Foreign Service officers and two contractors, former Navy SEALs, prompted multiple inquiries by the US House Oversight Committee on State Department security contracting procedures. The State Department's choice of a small private company for security, over a more well-known PSC with proven capabilities, related to the recent ban passed by Libyan interim authorities targeting international PSCs in the region. 'Federal contract data shows that the Benghazi security contract, worth up to $783,284, was listed as a 'miscellaneous' award, not as part of the large master State Department contract that covers protection for overseas embassies' (Ibidem).

The narrative in the employment of international PSCs in support of the Chinese investments is not focused on regime stabilization or changes, as in the Gaddafi case, but it still relies on critical PSC expertise in providing services not available from the hosting state. The killing of the American ambassador in Benghazi well underlines common threats that Chinese diplomats as well as SOE personnel may face along the BRI. In this respect the PSCs' services that are in dire need include essential aerial logistical support as well as utilization of scout drones, the employment of field doctors and nurses with capabilities in combat wound treatment and specialization in common local infections and diseases, as well as 'war geeks' that provide essential ITC capabilities in dangerous areas. Unfortunately, in China the common perception of PSCs' needs is still related to armoured vehicles and contractors showcasing heavy machine guns.

Since 2015, the amplified risks in the African continent include a wide spectrum of political and criminal violence: insurgent attacks, piracy, criminal extortion and kidnapping. One of the main differences from the experience drawn in the African continent compared with other BRI areas is that not only SOEs, but also private small- and medium-sized enterprises

(SMEs) operating small businesses have started to consider the employment of PSCs early on. The African market for force offers an interesting mix of capabilities ranging from the high-end spectrum of European, US and Israeli PSCs to the lower-end services of local tribal gunmen employed by Chinese small business owners. While the SOEs are increasingly conscious of the threats that their personnel will face, the willingness to pay has constrained the provision of high-level and very expensive security protection. Newly established Chinese security firms are trying to fill the gap by providing affordable yet professional services. Therefore, it is important to underline how the top Chinese PSCs have a price range that does not differ substantially from the international PSCs, but the middle- and lower-tier Chinese PSCs which compete with lower bid providing a lower efficiency don't understand this.

Several Chinese PSCs have made Africa their testing ground for overseas expansion. The anti-piracy business along Somali waters was one of the first cases in which Chinese PSCs overseas provided protection by escorting Chinese commercial vessels and oil tankers. Thanks to the international military mission that escorted the commercial vessels in the pirate infested area this business model is dwindling. However, the protection of Chinese infrastructure construction sites in the continent will sustain the demand for security services for years to come. An example is given by the road building projects carried out by the China Road and Bridge Corporation in Kenya, which counts on increasing support from the Dewei Security Group Ltd. (Lee 2014).

Although in Africa the market for force is overcrowded by local actors that are supported by the local government, the SOEs' preferential choice of Chinese security providers is linked with more trust in compatriots. Suspicion of African PSCs is motivated by the perception that the underpaid and underequipped operators could be part of the problem and not the solution. Therefore, the choice over an expensive international corporation and a cheaper Chinese PSC is quite straightforward. Another common perception among the SOE management is that Chinese PSCs can better preserve a company's business secrets than international counterparts, and that there is no cultural or language barrier in place. Another factor in favour of the Chinese PSC over the African is related to the fact that Chinese security operators are not entangled in tribal feuds or local political disputes.

According to Chinese national law, even in the African continent, Chinese PSC operators are forbidden to carry weapons, and in the case of the eruption of political or criminal violence, they are obliged to contact the nearest Chinese embassy or consulate, in order to coordinate a response with the local security forces. The lack of Chinese personnel carrying guns forces enhanced and advanced security measures, such as actionable intelligence gathering, and the necessity of nurturing Chinese experts in supervising local armed staff and the international contractors. Already, the leading Chinese PSCs with their headquarters in Beijing are supporting the hiring of Chinese linguists or Chinese managers with proven crisis management experience developed in the industrial sectors ranging from the hazardous chemical product plants to high-risk storage management.

3.10 Opportunities and Challenges: Private Security Companies' Monitoring and Governance

The analysis of the opportunities and challenges in the PSCs' employment drawn from the US, Russian and limited Chinese experience provides interesting insights that demystify commonly accepted perceptions in the market for force.

In the BRI narrative, financial opportunities are often overestimated, while challenges to the Chinese nationals abroad derived from criminal and political violence have been overlooked. Unfortunately, another fallacy that is going to affect the employment of PSCs along the BRI is the lack of proper government oversight.

China's central government is conscious that along the outbound investments security is not exclusively a domestic issue but a transnational problem. Besides being more focused on bilateral agreements instead of multilateral ones, China is relying on its own set of multilateral infrastructures from the SCO to AIIB in order to engage a broader set of actors in the establishment of procedures and enforcing capabilities. In this respect, China's revival of the Silk Road should be considered as a network of fluid trade links. The fluidity of the trade network is exemplified by the fact that there is not an official map, and the number of countries and key areas are continuously being updated. Moreover, the Belt and Road itself is presented as an initiative and not as a strategy, in order to maintain the opportunity to steer the planning along the way. Following this narrative, the employment of Chinese PSCs instead of the PLA or PAP in support of the BRI security network is perceived to preserve China 'peaceful rise' image. PSCs offer several degrees of deniability as they create a gap between contracting governments and final employers. In the specific case of Chinese

PSCs that employ only Chinese personnel there are still doubts about probable links with the PLA. Nevertheless, the BRI is catalysing the transformation of the Chinese market for force. The experience gained in cooperating with international PSCs is going to benefit the Chinese PSC in terms of technology transfer and human resources capacity building. At the same time, the employment of Chinese PSCs' rapid growth is still largely unregulated and under ineffective control.

The utility of PSCs should not be overlooked but at the same time the myth of economic efficiency has to be deflated in consideration of the higher costs for proper monitoring and control. In November 2007, the US independent Commission on Army Acquisition and Program Management in Expeditionary Operations report[35] released guidelines on PSC contracting opportunities and challenges. Subsequently, the US Army's Special Inspector General for Iraqi Reconstruction (SIGIR) report[36] released a comprehensive study that takes into account the cost of managing the market for force from the government point of view. The SIGIR report findings underline how the US military lacks the capacity for oversight and control of its contractors. In this respect, the main fallacy is related to the contracting officer representative in charge of the bidding and management process. The contracting officers' limited experience in the field increased the PSCs potential to avoid controls. While the US Department of Defence (DOD) after several years of experience on the ground in managing hundreds of PSCs that amount to thousands of contractors is still struggling with internal management capabilities and need for qualified government personnel, China and the SOEs have not yet started to build a pool of qualified contracting officials.

> The old cliché, money is power, could prove a useful touchstone in arriving at a first answer to this question. Defense controlled the contracting for the Iraq Security Forces Fund ($20.19 billion), the Commander's Emergency Response Program ($4.12 billion), and the bulk of contracting for the Iraq Relief and Reconstruction Fund ($20.86 billion). Thus, it held decisive sway over $45 billion (87%) of the roughly $52 billion allocated to the five major rebuilding funds that supported Iraq's reconstruction—most of which addressed security priorities through 2008 (see Figure 3.2).8 In Iraq, if money was power, and power determined who was in charge, then Defense was in charge.[37]

With respect to the private security sector in Iraq, a SIGIR quarterly report released in 2008 investigated the PSCs efficiency in protecting

US government, facilities and workers. The report identified 77 PSCs while the Congressional Budget Office estimated the presence of 25,000–30,000 security contractors. Shortly, another report from the Government Accountability Office affirmed that reliable data on the number of armed contractors was unavailable.

Since September 2007, 'Baghdad Bloody Sunday', involving state's security defence, and state managed to improve the oversight of PSCs establishing the following guidelines[38]:

- Armed Contractor Oversight Division to monitor PSCs and serve as the prime point of contact on PSC policies
- Increase in military units' responsibility for overseeing PSC missions, managing incidents, conducting investigations and executing contract management
- Liaison officers' training to monitor PSCs

The first two recommendations are not entirely applicable to the BRI context in which the Chinese PSCs are not flanked with the PLA, nor are they under the hosting country military supervision. Then the last recommendation is a priority that Beijing needs to take into serious account and start to build an adequate control and coordination structure.

The accepted model of the state monopoly on violence is sliding back to a pre-Westphalia situation, and China's increased demand for security hopefully will drive oversight and accountability.

As already mentioned, the benefits in the use of PSCs applied to the specific need for the BRI could be summarized as follows:

- Rapidity to deploy and adapt to the BRI fluidity and fast-changing environment
- Avoidance of the PLA and PAP presence when not specifically requested by the hosting country
- Support the overstretched MFA capabilities and human resource limits in foreign countries
- Assistance to the SOEs' lack of in-house security capabilities

As it happened in the United States, Beijing needs to evaluate how the rapid expansion of the market for force has led to lowering of standards both in the quality of personnel employed and in the services provided.

Notes

1. Reports of China's losses in Libya are inaccurate, said Shen Danyang, spokesman of the Ministry of Commerce, on Wednesday. China does not have direct investments in Libya, only contract projects, he said. 'No direct Chinese investments in Libya', *China Daily* August 25, 2011, http://www.chinadaily.com.cn/business/2011-08/25/content_13193258.htm
2. Circular n16 (2006) Circular n225 (2008), Circular n16 '*Interim measures for the supervision and* administration *of overseas State-owned assets of central State-owned Enterprises*' (2011).
3. Author's interview with international PSCs in Shanghai, November 2015.
4. 'Sudanese petroleum minister Mohamed Zayed Awad said that Chinese companies control 75 percent of foreign investment in Sudan's oil sector.'
5. 'The government had requested $1.9 billion from the Chinese government to develop oil fields and infrastructure projects. Part of the funds could be used to reopen key oil fields in Unity state that has been shut down since a civil war began in December 2013.' *Sudan Tribune*, 'South Sudan seeks nearly $2 billion loan from China' August 9, 2016, http://www.sudantribune.com/spip.php?article59880
6. After 54 consecutive months of year-on-year falls, the producer price index (PPI) rose 0.1% year-on-year in the month, according to the National Bureau of Statistics (NBS) October 14, 2016.
7. Author interview with the Chinese Contractors Association, Beijing September 2016.
8. China National Petroleum Corporation (CNPC), China Petroleum and Chemical Corporation Limited (Sinopec) and China National Offshore Oil Corporation (CNOOC).
9. 'FDI on the Rebound.' The At Kearney Foreign Direct Investment Confidence Index 2016. https://www.atkearney.com/documents/10192/8064626/2016+A.T.+Kearney+Foreign+Direct+Investment+Confidence+Index%E2%80%93FDI+on+the+Rebound.pdf/e61ec054-3923-4f96-b46c-d4b4227e7606
10. General Debate of the 70th Session of the UN official transcript of the Statement by H.E. Xi Jinping, president of the People's Republic of China, https://gadebate.un.org/sites/default/files/gastatements/70/70_ZH_en.pdf
11. The State Council of the People's Republic of China 'President Xi delivers keynote speech at B20 summit in Hangzhou', http://english.gov.cn/news/top_news/2016/09/04/content_281475432981211.htm
12. In August 2016, the Chinese outbound direct investments reached US$118 billion with an increase of 61.8% on the previous year. Ministry of

Commerce, http://europe.chinadaily.com.cn/business/2016-08/17/content_26510134.htm Xinhua China 'Jan-July Outbound Direct Investments surges 61.8%, (August 17, 2016), http://english.gov.cn/archive/statistics/2016/08/17/content_281475419422422.htm

13. 'Xi said that the military must never get stuck in its old ways. It needed to change with the times. China's military needs to put more focus on technology rather than force of numbers.' Xinhua Shanghai Daily. 'Army must change with the times' December 5, 2016, http://www.shanghaidaily.com/nation/Army-must-change-with-the-times/shdaily.shtml
14. Hua Chunying 'Remarks on Chinese Embassy in Kyrgyzstan Hit by Terrorist Attack. China strongly condemns the horrific terrorist attack against the Chinese Embassy in Kyrgyzstan. Terrorism is the common enemy for the international community, posing the gravest threat on regional countries. China also falls victim to terrorism. We will strengthen anti-terrorism cooperation with regional countries including Kyrgyzstan under bilateral and the Shanghai Cooperation Organization (SCO) frameworks, clamp down on all forms of terrorism, and take tangible efforts to ensure the safety of Chinese institutions and people in relevant countries and uphold regional peace and stability.' http://www.fmprc.gov.cn/mfa_eng/xwfw_665399/s2510_665401/t1393115.shtml
15. 'It is the possibility of Chinese dual-use bases in the IOR that deserves the most attention. A commercial facility with low-level logistical support capability, a dual-use base is a risk-free way of establishing maritime presence in a region of interest, Abhijit Singh A 'PLA-N' for Chinese maritime bases in the Indian Ocean, PacNet #7—CSIS newsletter January 26, 2015, https://www.csis.org/analysis/pacnet-7-%E2%80%98pla-n%E2%80%99-chinese-maritime-bases-indian-ocean
16. It refers to the Western and Japanese imperialism in China during 1839 and 1949. John King Fairbank 'The Cambridge History of China: Late Ch'ing, 1800–1911.' Cambridge University Press. 1978.
17. Professor Wang Yizhou, vice dean of the School of International Studies of Peking University, has initiated a new diplomatic concept—'creative involvement', calling on China to actively play a bigger role and voluntarily get involved in international affairs. Beijing Review 'A new direction for China political affairs' March 3, 2012, http://www.bjreview.com.cn/world/txt/2012-03/05/content_439626.htm
18. 'Absorb and Conquer. An EU Approach to Russian and Chinese Integration in Eurasia' European Council on Foreign Relations ECFR.EU May 2016.
19. Russian SEO Arms intermediary agency for defence products import/export, http://www.roe.ru/roe/eng_status.html
20. Chinese SEOs' defence sector manufacturers.

21. 'The commanders failed however to acknowledge the real lesson of Quetta: decades of Pakistani military and intelligence support underwritten by funding from quarters in Saudi Arabia for sectarian and ultra-conservative groups in Pakistan has divided the country almost irreversibly.' James M. Dorsey 'Political Violence and Sectarianism in Pakistan 'RSIS Commentary.
22. '"Soon we'll start hiring 700–800 police to be part of a separate security unit dedicated to Chinese security, and at a later stage a new security division would be formed," Jafer Khan, regional police officer in Gwadar told Reuters.' Syed Raza Hassan 'To protect Chinese investment, Pakistan military leaves little to chance' Reuters January 26, 2016, http://www.reuters.com/article/pakistan-china-security-gwadar-idUSKCN0VH06F
23. China 'New Normal' defines the transition from accelerated economic development of two digit GDP increase in the last three decades and a slower but steady economic development focused on 6–7% GDP growth per year.
24. 'The Pakistan military, which has detachments of civil, mechanical and electrical engineers, has had decades of experience with large infrastructure projects and analysts say the army is well placed to supervise the corridor.' *Financial Times* 'China urges Pakistan to give army lead role in Silk Road project. Squabbles in Islamabad highlight obstacles to Beijing's plans for transport and energy corridor' July 21, 2016, https://www.ft.com/content/5eea66c0-4ef9-11e6-8172-e39ecd3b86fc
25. In the last decade, Sino-Russian relations were considered to have reached a normalization stage based on pragmatic relationship eviscerated by any ideology driver, other than the common opposition to US unipolarity. Ibidem.
26. SCO sets blueprint for next decade, http://www.scosummit2012.org/english/2012-06/08/c_131640161.htm
27. 'Much like the inexact art of Kremlinology—divining the fortunes of the Soviet elite—Kazakhstan has produced its own parlor game of tracking the ups and downs of various political players.' Philip Shishkin, 'Central Asia Report', Asian Society (2012) p. 8.
28. Regional Anti-terrorist Structure (RATS), http://www.ecrats.com/en/normative_documents/2005
29. SCO members include China, Kazakhstan, Kyrgyzstan, Russia, Tajikistan and Uzbekistan, while Afghanistan, India, Iran, Mongolia and Pakistan are ranked as observers and Belarus, Turkey and Sri Lanka as dialogue partners.
30. With a reduced number of effectives than a normal division (around 7000 men among conscripts and contractors), the 201st motorized infantry division 'Gachinskaia' has been deployed in Tajikistan—under CIS mandate—in three military facilities near the capital Dushanbe since the end

of the Soviet-Afghan war. The last armoured personnel carrier that left Afghanistan in 1989 belonged to the 201st.
31. J.V. developed by Metallurgical Corporation of China and Jiangxi Copper Co. for an estimated investment of USD 3 billion.
32. Chinese vice minister of Commerce Gao Yan during the Second Meeting of China-Afghanistan Joint Committee of Economics and Trade in Beijing on 26 June 2015, http://english.mofcom.gov.cn/article/newsrelease/significantnews/201506/20150601027796.shtml
33. The number ranges from 26,000 to more than 40,000 depending on the reporting source.
34. Interview with Ethiopian security expert. Singapore, December 2015.
35. Also known as Gansler report 'Report of the Commission on Army Acquisition and Program Management in Expeditionary Operations' November 2007, http://psm.du.edu/media/documents/us_research_and_oversight/special_commissions/us_special_report_gansler.pdf
36. 'Learning From Iraq: A Final Report from the Special Inspector General for Iraq Reconstruction' culminates SIGIR's nine-year mission overseeing Iraq's reconstruction. It serves as a follow-up to our previous comprehensive review of the rebuilding effort, 'Hard Lessons: The Iraq Reconstruction Experience.' March 2013 Sigir website is close but the data can be found on https://cybercemetery.unt.edu/archive/sigir/20131001083907/http://www.sigir.mil/learningfromiraq/index.html
37. Ibidem.
38. Ibidem.

References

Arduino, A. 2015a. China–Central Asia: A New Economic, Security, and Logistic Network. In *China Power Asian Security*, ed. L.M. Routledge. Abingdon: Routledge.

———. 2015b. Chinese Private Security: A New Paradigm for Private Military and Counter-Terrorism? *Counter Terrorist Magazine*, 11.

———. 2015c. Security Privatization with Chinese Characteristics: The Role of Chinese Private Security Corporations in Protecting Chinese Outbound Investments and Citizens. *RSIS*, June. https://www.rsis.edu.sg/rsis-publication/idss/security-privatisation/#.Vi8fs64rK8U

———. 2017. China's Energy Interests in Central Asia and Russia: Symbiotic Distrust and Striking a Balance between Cooperation and Confrontation. In *China's Global Quest for Resources*, ed. F. Wu. Abingdon: Routledge.

Blank, S. 2006. *Russo-Chinese Energy Relations: Politics in Command*. London: GMB Publishing.

Bloomberg. 2013. China Eclipses US as the Biggest Trading Nation. *Bloomberg*, February 11. http://www.bloomberg.com/news/articles/2013-02-09/china-passes-u-s-to-become-the-world-s-biggest-trading-nation. Accessed 2016.

———. 2016. China's Digger Market Poised for Recovery Says Top Supplier. *Bloomberg*, July 20. Accessed 2017.

Cainey, A. 2016. Expectations Are High, Now the AIIB Has to Deliver. *Nikkei*, January 26. http://asia.nikkei.com/magazine/20160128-SHATTERED-HOPES/Politics-Economy/Andrew-Cainey-Expectations-are-high-now-the-AIIB-has-to-deliver

China Daily. 2016a. Africans See China Ties as a Benefit. *China Daily*, November 5–6.

———. 2016b. Key Part of Pakistan Economic Corridor Opens Up. *China Daily*, November 15.

———. 2016c. Sino-Thai Relations Boosted by $10.6b Rail Deal. *China Daily*, December 20. http://www.chinadaily.com.cn/world/2014livisitkst/2014-12/20/content_19130730.htm

China Military.com. 2017. Chinese Peacekeeping Infantry Battalion in S. Sudan Passes Equipment Inspection. *China Military*, February 2. http://eng.chinamil.com.cn/view/2017-02/03/content_7474939.htm. Accessed 2017.

Eder, T. 2014. *China-Russia Relations in Central Asia: Energy Policy, Beijing's New Assertiveness and 21st Century Geopolitics.* Wiesbaden: Springer Fachmedien.

Erickson, A.S. 2016. China's Blueprint for Sea Power. *Jamestown Foundation China Brief Volume*: 16 Issue (July 11). https://jamestown.org/program/chinas-blueprint-for-sea-power/

Eva Dou, R.C. 2014. Behind Vietnam's Anti-China Riots, a Tinderbox of Wider Grievances Investigation Reveals Deeper Troubles Brewing in a Country Where Officials Usually Quash Protests. *Wall Street Journal*, June 17. http://www.wsj.com/articles/behind-vietnams-anti-china-riots-a-tinderbox-of-wider-grievances-1403058492. Accessed 2015.

Hastings, M. 2010. The Runaway General. *The Rolling Stone*, June 22. http://www.rollingstone.com/politics/news/the-runaway-general-20100622. Accessed 2016.

Hobson, P. 2016. Russia, Pakistan, China Warn of Increased Islamic State Threat in Afghanistan. *Reuters*, December 27. http://in.reuters.com/article/afghanistan-taliban-russia-pakistan-chin-idINKBN14G19H?feedType=RSS&feedName=southAsiaNews. Accessed 2017.

ICG. 2015. Kazakhstan's Protests Postponed—But for How Long? *Crisisgroup.org*, May 12. http://blog.crisisgroup.org/europe-central-asia/kazakhstan/2016/05/12/kazakhstans-protests-postponed-but-for-how-long/. Accessed 2017.

Kabraji, R. 2012. The China-Pakistan Alliance: Rhetoric and Limitations. *Chatham House*, December. https://www.chathamhouse.org/sites/files/chathamhouse/public/Research/Asia/1212pp_kabraji.pdf. Accessed 2015.

Keaten, J. 2007. Denard, Infamous Mercenary and Self-Styled 'Pirate', Dies at 78. *The Independent Associated Press*, October 15. http://www.independent.co.uk/news/world/europe/denard-infamous-mercenary-and-self-styled-pirate-dies-at-78-396897.html. Accessed 2016.

Lee, K. 2014. Chinese Private Security Firms Go Overseas: Crossing the River by Feeling the Stones. *African Monitor*, September 8.

Lim, S. 2013. *China and Japan in the Russian Imagination, 1685–1922: To the Ends of the Orient*. London: Routledge.

Mathieu Duchatel, O.B. 2014. Mathieu Duchatel, Oliver Brauner and Zhou Hang Protecting China's Overseas Interests. The Slow Shift away from Non-interference. *SIPRI Policy Paper* 41 Cap.2, June.

Page, J. 2016. China Builds First Overseas Military Outpost. *Wall Street Journal*, August 19. Accessed 2016.

Pantucci, R. 2017. China Expanding Security Role in Afghanistan. *Reuters*, March 1. http://www.reuters.com/article/china-afghanistan-securityrole-idUSKBN1683QY. Accessed 2017.

Portyakov, V. 2006. The Russian Vector in Global Chinese Migration. *Far Eastern Affairs* 34 (1): 47–61.

Price, G. 2011. China Pakistan Relations. *ECRAN Background Brief*, February 15. http://eeas.europa.eu/archives/docs/china/docs/division_ecran/ecran_is1_china_pakistan_relations_gareth_price_en.pdf. Accessed 2015.

Reuters. 2010. Afghanistan Orders Ban on Private Security Firms. *Reuters*, August 17. http://www.reuters.com/article/us-afghanistan-security-idUSTRE67G1ZP20100817. Accessed 2015.

———. 2017. For Benghazi Diplomatic Security, U.S. Relied on Small British Firm. *Reuters*. http://www.reuters.com/article/us-libya-usa-bluemountain-idUSBRE89G1TI20121018

Rikelton, C. 2014. Kyrgyzstan: Chinese Workers Deported After Riot at Strategic Refinery. *Eurasianet*, July 3. http://www.eurasianet.org/node/68856. Accessed 2017.

Singapore Today. 2015. Singapore Today 'Preventing the Next Tianjin Incident in China. *Today Online*, November. http://m.todayonline.com/chinaindia/china/preventing-next-tianjin-incident-china

Singer, P. 2007. *Corporate Warriors: The Rise of the Privatized Military Industry*. Cornell Studies in Security Affairs.

The Economist. 2017. Sri Lankans Protest Against Chinese Investment. *The Economist*, January. http://www.economist.com/news/asia/21714374-its-one-way-pay-debts-china-sri-lankans-protest-against-chinese-investment. Accessed 2017.

The Guardian. 2016. Dozens of Workers Dead in China Power Plant Collapse. *The Guardian*, November 24. http://www.theguardian.com/world/2016/nov/24/workers-dead-china-power-plant-collapse

Wang, Y. 2016. Top Belt, Road Collaborators Ranked. *China Daily*, October 29–30.

Weits, R. 2015. Beijing Waivers on Afghanistan Security Commitment. *CACI Analyst*, September 2. http://www.cacianalyst.org/publications/analytical-articles.html. Accessed 2016.

Xin Hua. 2014. Chinese President Proposes Asia-Pacific Dream. *Xinhua Net*, November 9. http://news.xinhuanet.com/english/china/2014-11/09/c_133775812_2.htm. Accessed 2015.

———. 2015. Xi Jinping—Strengthening Security Cooperation is in the Common Interests of China and Afghanistan. *Xinhua Net*, July 10. http://news.xinhuanet.com/english/2015-07/10/c_134401664.htm. Accessed 2016.

———. 2016. Chinese Dream Rejuvenating Country. *China Daily*, November 30. http://www.chinadaily.com.cn/cndy/2016-11/30/content_27521547.htm

Xinhua. 2013. Kashgar Killings. *Xinhua Net*, April 29. http://news.xinhuanet.com/english/china/2013-04/29/c_132349219.htm. Accessed 2015.

———. 2016. UN Chief Slams Killing of Two UN Chinese Peacekeepers in South Sudan Fighting. *China Daily*, July 12. http://www.chinadaily.com.cn/world/2016-07/12/content_26052773.htm

Yang, Z. 2016. Zhang Yang SCO Members Will Join Forces to Combat Terrorism. *Shanghai Daily*, December 5.

Zhou, B. 2015. *Safeguarding China's Overseas Interests Through Military Cooperation.*

CHAPTER 4

Globalization and the Market for Force

Abstract Beijing's economic influence in shaping international institutions is yet to be seen in the market for force. Nevertheless the Chinese insurance sector began to realize the importance of this business niche. Traditional static security, counter-terrorism as well as kidnapping for ransom are going to provide important contracts along the Belt and Road Initiative (BRI). As it happened in the US war efforts, China is learning an important lesson: the private security companies' (PSCs) employment practices offer short-term flexibility and economic benefits but also could produce long-term negative spillovers if not properly contained. New businesses that the Chinese private security sector is looking into are related to the protection of macro-cities and the international hunt for corrupted officials, who had fled the country in an attempt to escape with the embezzled sums.

Keywords Special insurance • K&R • SOEs' risk • BRI security

4.1 China Vs. US Market for Force

He who wishes to fight must first count the cost. Sun Zi, *The Art of War* (Cap II)

The market for force evolution is witnessing new actors and stages: from the US Army as the main client to Chinese Belt and Road Initiative (BRI) and Russian proxy armies.

© The Author(s) 2018

A. Arduino, *China's Private Army*,
https://doi.org/10.1007/978-981-10-7215-4_4

Beijing's economic influence in shaping international institutions is yet to be seen in the market for force. Nevertheless the Chinese insurance sector began to realize the importance of this business niche. Traditional static security, counter-terrorism as well as kidnapping for ransom are going to provide important contracts along the BRI. According to the Hiscox Group's conservative estimate, more than US$500 million a year goes to criminal gang of kidnappers, mostly in South America. Recently, Chinese insurance experts began to acknowledge the role of prevention in this line of business. Notwithstanding the market for force renaissance, in both the United States and China the role of private security companies (PSCs) is in dire need for a clear definition. The lack of checks and balances allows the PSCs to operate in a grey area easily exploited. Also, the market for force benefits is constrained by ineffective oversight and control.

From the end of the Cold War to the dawn of the Iraqi and Afghan conflicts, the market for force has followed the demands of one client, the United States.

Due to its conduct in these two conflicts:

> The United States has opened the proverbial Pandora's box, releasing mercenarism back into international affairs. Now that the industry is back and unlikely to go away anytime soon. (McFate 2014)

The post–Cold War security vacuum has influenced China's posture in international affairs. The BRI, with the rise of China as one of the world's leading economies, is becoming a major provider for a broad range of security services.

China's resource to the BRI available to be invested overseas reaches US$51.1 billion.[1] This amount of money is influencing the market for force in different directions from the patterns previously established by the United States. In this respect, China, compared to the United States, is not engaged in large-scale conflicts and does not have at present a necessity to outsource logistical and infrastructural services in war zones.[2]

Therefore, Beijing's first requirement is to assure adequate security to the state-owned enterprises (SOEs) that wish to establish ventures in fragile states. While it seems clear that China's growing economic might is actively influencing political outcomes, with special regard to the neighbouring countries, the role of Chinese SOEs as the main contractors for Chinese and international PSCs does not seem to be linked with a hidden political agenda for the moment.[3]

Nevertheless, examples of Beijing's economic influence in shaping international institutions are already common, ranging from the support to Association of Southeast Asian Nations (ASEAN) members or Central Asian countries to avoid multilateral confrontations (Xinhua 2016). Therefore, in the near future there is a remote possibility that Chinese PSCs could leverage their capabilities in pressuring weaker actors to adapt to Beijing will.

The global financial crisis (2007–2008) and the rebalancing of US and European Union (EU) forces in Afghanistan and in the Middle East (2014) have subsequently diminished the demands for PSC employment by the West. Following the exponential growth of the sector since the two Gulf Wars,[4] the temporary shrinking of the market for force has been counterbalanced by new threats and new business opportunities. New conflicts, such as Syria and Yemen, have generated a renewed demand for mercenaries, which has ignited the surge of new PSCs that are linked with international alliances in the area.

The Russian Federation undertook employment of Russian PSCs in the area before openly supporting the Assad regime with aerial bombing and military advice. Moreover, the United Arab Emirates (UAE) deployed South American contractors of the size of a battalion, mainly from Colombia, for use in the ongoing Yemen conflict. The role of the South American unit, overseen by the founder of Blackwater Erik Prince (Mazzetti and Hager 2011) and managed by the UAE company Reflex Responses,[5] was supposed to be more in line with the other PSCs' passive stance in the area: to protect the oilfields or, in the case of dire need, to quell local riots. Contrary to the previsions and with no more apparent connection with Erik Prince, the call for arms in the Yemen conflict led the UAE Army to employ the contractors as a quick-reaction force (Hager and Mazzetti 2015).

Furthermore, a new breed of PSC and international corporations with a PSC spin-off has mushroomed after the second Iraq War and the rampant increase of terrorist threats. The counter-terrorist efforts as well as the Western fear for imminent attacks on the civilian population have led several PSCs to adapt their business model to this new market. Nevertheless, Western countries' shrinking economies could not sustain the budgets that supported the PSCs' growth during the previous conflicts. At the same time, the growth of the Middle East and the Chinese security market budgets are not an equal match to the former US one. Therefore, international PSC competition to enter into the new markets, especially China, is fierce. Securing a Chinese PSC partner in order to operate more freely in the Chinese regulatory limbo, without being perceived as a wholly owned foreign enterprise, is especially beneficial. This competition strikes several commonalities with the first wave of multinational corporations in the early 1980s, which were eager to accept any kind of partnership with local Chinese actors just to gain a foothold in the opening Chinese market. Moreover, a coherent approach to the use of PSCs in China is going to be influenced not only by the SOEs but also by the Chinese Ministry of Foreign Affairs (MFA). The MFA is increasingly under pressure to be accountable for overseas Chinese workers and tourists. This difficult task is going to force Beijing to actively influence the regulations of PSC partnerships and deployments.

Another point of divergence with the US model is related to the profound differences between the two military industry complexes (MICs). In the United States, the MIC cast its powerful influence on the US Army and by reflection on the PSCs that operate on the Department of Defence and the Department of State accounts. Also, the US Army uses a wide array of high-technology weapons. Therefore, the new weapon systems' platforms allow for service outsourcing that is contracted most of the time to the same manufacturer that produced the system. In this respect, the MIC and PSC boards of directors comprise a wide assortment of former military and government officials in the so-called revolving door between corporate managers and government officials in Washington. The case of the former Blackwater board of directors could be an example in having the former CIA coordinator for counter-terrorism Cofer Black as vice chairman of the group during the years 2004 and 2008. But the corporations that benefited the most during the latest conflicts could count on even higher former US government officials in their corporate structure. For instance, the former Halliburton Group CEO Dick Cheney (from 1995 to 2000) became the vice president of the United States during the George W. Bush administration.

While four of the top ten arms-producing companies are in Europe, the combined sales total of the US MIC almost surpass the EU sales compounded together. According to the latest figures released in 2016 by the Stockholm International Peace Research Institute (SIPRI), world military expenditures totalled almost US$1.7 trillion in 2015, an increase of 1% in real terms from 2014. The increase reflects an overall growth in Asia and Oceania, Central and Eastern Europe.[6] Despite a reduction in defence spending in 2015, the United States remains in the leading position in 2015 with $596 billion, followed by China's expenditure of $215 billion.

The main difference is that the US spending decreased by 2.4% in absolute terms, while Chinese spending soared by 7.4% from 2014 to 2015. According to SIPRI analysis, the United States consistently tops their charts as the world's leading arms manufacturer and exporter.

In this respect, the US MIC's supremacy lies in the fact that it is the major arms supplier for NATO countries. Also non-NATO allies rely on US arms manufacturing for an important part of their defence needs. Nevertheless, the Chinese MIC is not waiting on the bench. Following President Xi's call for the modernization of the Chinese army, several Chinese defence groups ranging from Poly Group to Norinco are raising their production and sales capabilities. Since the policy of opening up promoted by Deng Xiaoping in the late 1970s, the Chinese defence sector has been proactive in the use of imported dual-use technologies as well as the civil-military-industrial sector integration, in order to reduce the technological gap (Lague and Zhu 2012).

> The long-term goal is to transform some of the leading contractors, such as China State Shipbuilding Corporation (CSSC), Aviation Industry Corporation of China (AVIC) and China Aerospace Science and Industry Corporation into homegrown versions of American giants Lockheed Martin and Northrop Grumman or Britain's BAE Systems.

In this respect, Chinese military spending alone is not going to help the overall MIC modernization, mainly due to the fact that the PRCs' high-end technological weapon platforms are still based on foreign technologies and expertise. Additionally, Russia (Barabanov et al. 2012) remains the preferred partner for high-end weapon technology transfers especially in the aircraft engine field as well as in high-end surface-to-air missile defence.[7] Nevertheless, the question of when China reaches the sophistication level of its Russian counterpart is not a matter of if but when. The new direction imposed on the Chinese MCI public and growing private sector is already witnessing a paradigm shift from low-end ammunition and weapons bulk manufacturing to the development of fifth-generation aircraft fighters or area denial ballistic missiles (Farley 2015). One of the most active MCI segments is the military shipbuilding sector that is benefitting from the growth of the mainland civilian shipbuilding capacity and technological advancement derived from joint ventures with foreign partners.

After two decades of increases in military spending, the Chinese MCI is witnessing the growth of the private sector together with the SOEs.

Whether the involvement of the private Chinese security sector is a positive multiplier is yet to be proven. At the moment, compared to the United States, the Chinese links between the MCI private security sector and PSCs are, at best, weak. In this regard the limited capabilities of the Chinese PSCs and the restraints on carrying weapons abroad do not provide the necessary business volume to meet the MCI sector's interests.

> In response to the new requirement coming from the country's growing strategic interests, the armed forces will actively participate in both regional and international security cooperation and effectively secure China's overseas interests. And in response to the new requirement arising from China's all-round and deepening reform, the armed forces will continue to follow the path of civil-military integration (CMI), actively participate in the country's economic and social construction, and firmly maintain social stability, so as to remain a staunch force for upholding the CPC's ruling position and a reliable force for developing socialism with Chinese characteristics. (State Council Information Office of the People's Republic of China 2015)

As stated in the People's Liberation Army's (PLA) 2013 and 2015 white papers, the army's capability to project power overseas is still in dire need of modernization. At the same time, the Chinese capabilities in non-combatant evacuations have already reached high standards. While the PLA and People's Armed Police (PAP) are going to increase their capabilities to protect Chinese Overseas Direct Investments, Chinese PSCs are at the challenge's forefront. While Chinese reliance on PSCs is increasing, it is still far from the US model in which private contractors implement core security interests. In this respect, selected PLA specialists protect Chinese MFA officials. In classic socialist tradition, all the personnel assigned to Chinese embassies and consulates, including the drivers, must be Chinese. The same tradition is still carried on in Russian Federation diplomatic outposts. On the contrary, during the Iraq and Afghan conflicts, US Foreign Service senior officials including Ambassador Paul Bremer, head of the Coalition Provisional Authority in Iraq (Gallagher and Del Vecchio 2014) and the former Afghan president Hamid Karzai utilized contractors for close security protection.

Nevertheless, profit maximization is the silver lining that connects Chinese and American market for force's privatization.

Both kinds of PSCs provide security services in order to increase their profits and market share. The US and other Western corporations during the last decades were almost dependent on a monopolistic client, the US

Department of Defence. Similarly, the Chinese PSCs' main SOE clients are creations of the Chinese state apparatus. Therefore, both markets are characterized by close links between public and private sectors. In the US case, all contracts and licencing must be approved by the State Department's Office of Defence and Trade Controls (ODTC), while in China the government body in charge of licencing and approval is the National Development Reform Commission (NDRC),[8] the MFA and MOD. All these government bodies have a say on the matter, but none has a definitive veto power.

As it happened in the US war efforts, China is learning an important lesson: the PSCs' employment practice offers short-term flexibility and economic benefits but also can produce long-term negative spillovers if not properly contained.

In this respect, China's business and security-specific needs are related to the peculiar culture that embeds the Chinese SOEs. The 'Chinese characteristics' that permeate China's political and business culture are going to affect the security market's demand and supply. One of the key factors is directly related to the size of the Chinese foreign direct investment (FDI). While Chinese expertise in the security sector is still improving, the Chinese SOEs' capabilities in building infrastructures and the availability of funds from Chinese banks are unmatched.

Contrary to the US model, the utility of private force for China could be summarized in the following. Chinese PSCs:

- Fill a gap in the provision of high-security services
- Provide on-demand force that is not already available locally
- Transfer security technologies and capabilities
- Add a layer of plausible deniability to the BRI win-win narrative
- Promote loss avoidance within the PLA's 'one-child' army

In this respect, international and local Chinese corporations are going to be the first to understand that the markets for the new dynamics for force-on-demand are going to produce massive profits.[9] The large number of Chinese PSCs present on the internal market does not match the expectations of the international market. At the moment, foreign corporations and professional supply the needed Chinese expertise. The one-stop shop for special insurance, risk assessment and mitigation as well as crisis management operators in Mainland China is not there yet. Nevertheless, the business turnover expected in the security market along the BRI is already forcing fast-paced changes and professionalization. Expectations for mature sectors range from five years (Chinese think tanks) to a more reasonable ten years of time frame.

One factor that is often deemed not relevant with the reform of the state monopoly of force is related to the new Chinese demographic compared to the recent past. While PLA doctrine and strategies were focused on waves of soldiers storming the front, the present reality is a military force composed almost entirely by the only son in a family. Over 35 years, the one-child policy, enacted in order to avoid an uncontrolled demographic explosion, has forced the security sector to take into consideration how the loss of the only child is producing stringent grievances against the state. The propaganda of the heroes sacrificed for the motherland is less convincing than in the past when joining the PLA was considered a chance to get a lifetime occupation and improved social status.[10] Despite the relaxation of the one-child law in 2016, the rapid ageing of the Chinese population compounded with more than three decades of the one-child policy is already placing constraints on how the central government is expected to react in the case the soldier's death. This social trend is also influencing the search for talent by Chinese PSCs with special regards to young graduates with foreign language or cross-cultural management capabilities. The family expectations for the only children are related to having safe jobs in mainland, possibly not too far from the old parents' home than a dangerous job in Kabul.

The growth of China, which as a leading economic power has brought about new dynamics in the geopolitical sphere, is influencing the new structure of the international system. This role, which has characterized the employment of PSCs in the last five decades, is going to be affected by China's economic assertiveness. The international security environment is already transforming due to a growing unease due to the perception of a Chinese threat. Moreover, the private security dynamics that are mainly influenced by market requests are facing a deep shift from West to East, in terms of deals and partnerships (Global Times 2015). The 'market economy with Chinese characteristics' is quite different from the stage to which international private security actors are accustomed. Since the 1990s, the market economy justification for the employment of PSC was the rationale behind the private efficiency versus the public one. During the Thatcher-Reagan period, the trends behind the New Public Management (NPM) were summarized by the '3 Es'—economy, efficiency and effectiveness (Moore 1995)—three dimensions in which the private sphere was supposed to be better in managing the provision of public services. Therefore, an important part of the state NPM has been related to the privatization of hospitals, schools, public utilities and even detention facilities. Looking at the Chinese dimension, the reform towards government efficiency in the public sector has been enacted in several areas, but the growth of bigger SOEs labelled 'national champions'[11] does not envisage a trend towards 'small is beautiful' for the private sector. The Western perception of inefficiency of the public sector, even in the management of force, has been one of the mainstream reasons used to justify the use of PSCs. However, Chinese reasoning in the use of PSC has to be seen under different lenses, including the need to upgrade management expertise in the use of force by exposing local actors to foreign best practices. While the overall PSC sector reform and development is still at a start-up phase, several other security and risk management capabilities are reaching their maturity.

In this respect, China has already showcased an increasing crisis management capability in the evacuation of Chinese nationals from dangerous zones, as in Libya in 2011 and more recently in Yemen. In this latest crisis, a joint effort between Chinese diplomatic missions in the area and the PLA's Navy (PLAN) warships operating in the Gulf of Aden secured hundreds of Chinese nationals and then transferred them from Yemen to Djibouti. The frigates Linyi, Weifang and several other support vessels that were employed in anti-piracy missions near Somalia were diverted to Yemen in the evacuation effort. The growing role of the Chinese PLAN in the area is symbolized by the fact that the two frigates docked in a foreign port during the Yemen evacuation and the missile frigate *Xuhou* provided long-range support to the ships evacuating Chinese nationals from Libya. In addition to the already-mentioned protection of structures and personnel, the rise of new terrorist threats has also increased the role of PSCs in the delivery of security services and transfer of tactical capabilities. Referring to possible terrorist actions, China could benefit from the expertise that several American or Israeli PSCs provide in the training of air marshals. Meanwhile, UK and Singaporean PSCs and insurance companies, specialized in anti-piracy, will be able to transfer best practices that enable Chinese PSCs to cooperate with the PLAN task force that was already operating from the Somali coast to the Malacca Straits.

Whereas China's defence spending has increased steadily over the past few years averaging 2%[12] of its GDP (in absolute terms with a double-digit increase per year), it is more difficult to track the expenditure incurred by

SOEs in private security. Proxy figures related to the operational cost of international PSCs could be used to infer the capital involved, but the lack of transparency in China's accounting practices constrains this exercise to merely an educated guess. In this respect, the market for force is not an open market in a strict economic sense as the asymmetry of information between the principal/actor is mostly in favour of the latter. Moreover, if analysing both the Chinese and the US market for force, one common mistake is to perceive security as a pure commodity. Security and the use of force is a commodity that is not strictly demand driven due to the fact that the asymmetry between the service providers and the clients could lead to market distortion. In this case, the market distortion is related not only to costly economic inefficiencies but also to the loss of lives and the perpetuation of insecurity and weak states. Therefore, several cases in post-colonial African conflicts showcased unscrupulous mercenaries that promoted a constant state of fear in order continue selling their services (Brooks 2002). For example, in the 1980s the lack of accountability in Angola and Sierra Leone allowed executive outcomes (EO) to perpetrate a series of crimes ranging from an attempted coup to a variety of human rights violations. Also, on several occasions, the PSCs' profit-driven strategy diverges from the public one. The heavily armoured private security convoys escorting American diplomats or high-ranking official along the 'Irish Route' (Rayment 2005) in Baghdad have triggered an incredible amount of weapons discharged on civilian vehicles that were only riding too near to the convoy. While most of the time the rules of engagement were respected from the PSCs' side, the impact on the local population made the Coalition Army's efforts to win the hearts and the minds even more difficult.

Therefore, the friction point is generated when the PSC substitutes or overlaps the provision of services that previously were only delivered by national armed forces and law enforcement agencies. Hence, the unregulated shareholder-stakeholder conflict of interest is at the origin of numerous problems linked with the employment of PSCs. Furthermore, the use of force in a private capacity could be channelled to fulfil hidden agendas inside the contracting company—diverging from the headquarters or the state's own international policy—or even by the same PSC that could profit by the continuance of the status quo. Recently, the Iraq and Afghanistan conflicts have highlighted how PSCs are a double-edged sword. On the one side, the PSC enables the war effort by giving support to the state's army. On the other side, the PSC damages the state legitimacy with the killing of innocent civilians and the 'above the law' attitude.

In July 2016, then secretary of defence Robert Gates delivered a speech at the Economic Club of Chicago which emphasized that the US military should be prepared 'to win the wars we are in while being prepared for threats on or beyond the horizon'. The new mentality is a return on the past focus on 'small wars' that characterized the nineteenth century, when minor conflicts were waged far from the Western borders. Procrastination in the Iraq, Afghanistan conflicts and the recent one in Sudan, have opened new markets and diversified the chance for growth not only for international PSCs but also for local ones that have mushroomed to provide subcontracting services. In several occasions, former local contractors employed by international PSCs have created local companies that provide security services for a fraction of the price (Spear 2006). These companies with personnel that range from Africa to Colombia are now trying to reach the Chinese market counting on one factor that well suits the Chinese SOEs, affordability.

While the private market for force is a new spring season, both in the United States and China, the role of PSCs is in dire need for a clear definition. The lack of a mutually agreed definition of checks and balances allows the PSC to operate in a legal limbo that is prone to abuse (Siebels 2014). Actually, the current self-imposed code of conduct established by international operators is quite far from an internationally agreed framework of law that could lead to an effective and efficient public–private partnership.[13] Besides the common problems related to the enforcement of a voluntary code of conduct in precarious international situations where the rule of law is non-existent, the evolution of the International Code of Conduct (ICoC) from the first draft agreed under the so-called Montreux Document on private military and security companies[14] provides a positive trend that could be followed by Chinese stakeholders. During the employment of DynCorp by the US Department of State in 1991, in order to support the Colombian government in the efforts to eradicate the drug plantation, the US government granted immunity to the contractors. At that time, the US government had institutionalized a dangerous trend, immunity for contractors. This trend was soon legally defined in the notorious Order 14 of the Coalition Provisional Authority in Iraq and subsequently in Afghanistan, granting to PSCs immunity from the laws of the host country. Not having yet faced the prosecution of Chinese citizens involved in PSC activities abroad, the Chinese legal system has not yet been tested on this ground.

In this respect, China is poised to increase the use of PSCs, influencing marked demands and outcomes, hence the necessity to engage Beijing in the creation of an agreed international framework of laws and regulations:

- Establishing clear procedures and bidding vetting mechanisms
- Promoting information exchanges
- Developing a chain of accountability
- Endorsing an oversight and enforcement mechanism
- Avoiding the pitfall of granting immunity to contractors via bilateral agreements

Besides the scarcity of complete and reliable information on the structure and scope of a PSC as well as the lack of financial transparency, it is critical to take into account the role of PSC not as an individual entity but as a part of a complex network that entangles public and private actors on a global stage. The complex dynamic system in which the PSC operates is continuously evolving, and only a non-linear approach could be employed in framing a commonly agreed PSC definition. Focusing on a single component, without taking in to account the continuous interaction of the parts could promote bias and flawed perspectives.

> The privatization of security serves different goals and actors. For first world countries it is a way of avoiding putting their own soldiers and material at risk. (…) For governments in weak state it is a possibility to secure their position and enhance inner as well as external security. For TNC especially in the extractive branch, it is necessary to guard their investment in insecure areas. (…) Finally, the humanitarian community, which conducts a historically new global 'business', needs security to operate. (Kramer 2007)

While it is still important to stress on the difference between the employment of Chinese PSCs as a defensive force to protect FDI and the US employment of PSC in the support of the war effort, it is not difficult to forecast how a Chinese PSC in the near future could ignite a crisis that the Chinese MFA will have to account for. Several crises could spawn from the excessive use of force in containing criminal extortion or managing the local workforce. At the same time, the killing of Chinese contractors and the spread in the Chinese social media (e.g. Weixin, Wechat, Douban[15]) of vivid images of mutilated bodies could ignite a wave of protests at home

(Tatlow 2015) against the Chinese foreign policy of non-interference.[16] An example is given by the operation Phantom Fury (November 2004) in which the US Army recaptured the city of Fallujia with a high rate of casualties on both sides. The operation had been pushed forward after the commotion caused by the killing and public displays of the disfigured bodies of four American Blackwater contractors. The main rationale of the operation was not related to a broader strategic manoeuvre but to stem the rise of an outraged public opinion back home.

4.2 China Vs. Russia Market for Force

> In other words, we are not talking of a typical western PMC charged with guarding a power plant in Afghanistan or Iraq, what appears to be in the making is a professional intervention force controlled by the state and used to advance Russian interest outside the country. At the same time such a force would be deniable at the outset of any intervention. (Worcester 2014)

From the Russian standpoint, the role given in the military doctrine to proxy warfare has not changed since the time of the Soviet Union, only the actors. Currently, Russia is unable to count on former Soviet satellite states to provide the proxy forces enabling power projection for political and economic interest abroad. The annexation of Crimea and the hybrid conflict in Ukraine showcase how 'volunteers' and PSCs (ChVK in Russian) have replaced proxy armies such as the Cuban volunteers in the Angola Conflict (Gleijeses 2002). Nevertheless, the role of Russian PSCs is not only related to the protection of Russian energy companies abroad or in anti-piracy support on Russian commercial vessels, but it is going to have greater strategic value on the geopolitical chessboard. Prior to the official Kremlin intervention in Syria, the involvement of the Russian PSCs in the Middle East is still a matter of guesswork. Since the 1990s, the Russian local market for private force has been contained by the state in order to avoid heavily armed bodyguards in protection of oligarchs, roaming around Moscow with impunity. Furthermore, it is reported that the restrictions in the use of force are being gradually lifted, especially with regards to the private security forces contracted to protect the energy sector interest of state corporations such as Gazprom.[17]

Compared to the US counterpart, it is presumed that Russia started using PSCs in close cooperation with the military, but in a more subtle way due to the Russian law limitation that constrains the use of private armed personnel abroad. Albeit the employment of private contractors for deniable off the budget operations by the CIA in Iraq and Afghanistan (Zenko 2015), the 'Zero Footprint' role of the Russian PSC is more marked. At the same time, the need for plausible deniability from the Chinese side is considered minimum. The mercantilist blueprint of the BRI does not create worries over the fact that China is going to contract the US and Russian addiction to the employment of PSCs.

Quite similar to the Chinese law against nationals engaging in armed conflict for profit, mercenary activity is outlawed by the Russian criminal code.[18] Currently, the role and the partnership between the government and the private security sector is suspended in a legal limbo and the ample grey areas that characterize the regulations against the offer of mercenary services is circumvented by a series of international shell companies allegedly supported by the state information services such as the Russian military intelligence (GRU) and the better-recognized Federal Security Service of the Russian Federation (FSB).

According to Denis Korotkov investigative reports on contemporary Russian mercenaries and their role with the paramilitary groups in the Russian intervention in Ukraine and Syria (Gostev and Coalson 2016), the unregistered private military contracting agency called ChVK Vagner operates in Syria with heavily armed former Russian servicemen.

> Based on information coming out of Syria at first- or secondhand, the Vagner group is often used as elite infantry, which naturally leads to casualties much greater than special forces typically see. But who coordinates this work and who commands them, I don't know. (Fontanka 2016)

The Vagner mercenaries reportedly played an important role in helping the forces of Syrian President Bashar al-Assad recapture Palmyra. In addition, according to the Russian investigative reporter, the Russian defence ministry allegedly supplied to the PSC logistic airplanes and helicopters as well as distinctive weapons in use by the GRU special units. At the same time, it is possible to speculate that due to the high volume of Russian military hardware transferred to the area, it is not impossible to acquire the same equipment on the international arms market.

One of the main differences with the paramilitary units employed in Ukraine and the Vagner group is that former soldiers compose the latter. Another difference with the paramilitary volunteers is that the average age of the Russian PSC contractors is over 30 and comprises mostly veterans who have been gaining previous experience in official Russian-led conflicts. Also the main distinction with the Chinese and US counterpart is the high rate of casualties. The website militaryarms.ru reports that the Vagner forces are distinguished by their very high percentage of losses, being employed as shock troops in the most delicate areas of the conflict. While the US PSCs are entangled in the war effort and have to take a proactive stance in the use of force and the Chinese are still on the fringe of the active involvement, the perception of the use of Russian PSCs is that their employers consider them front-line troops.

Contrary to the US and the Chinese PSCs, the employment of Russian PSCs appears more related to minimizing political risks than maximizing the economic ones. During the Cold War, Moscow had already mastered the use of external forces that did not have a traceable connection to the Russian foreign policy. While the Russian Federation Army overall reform and strengthening process has been slowed down by the collapse of the oil prices, the role of Russian PSCs has grown not only as deniable force in promoting Moscow interest abroad but also as recipient of professional soldiers dismissed during the army's demobilization. Moscow, as well as Beijing, is concerned with the fact that a large number of demobilized soldiers could join the ranks of criminal gangs employing their former training in support of criminal activities. The main difference with the Chinese is related to the fact that most of the demobilized Russian forces are veterans with active combat experience.

At the same time, while several Western scholars still focus on the fact that there is a limited role of the market in the Russian PSCs expansion compared to the EU or the US counterparts, it is not improper to forecast their employment by foreign corporations that are in dire need of security in post-soviet spaces. One of the selling points of the Russian PSC RSB (Russian Security System) Group,[19] as reported on their website, is the fact that they offer a service to countries and corporations that could not feel comfortable in engaging Western security service providers. In the meantime, several Chinese PSCs that are involved in the protection of Chinese interests in the Central Asia part of the BRI are probing possible cooperation with Russian professionals, considering the fact the Russian language is still the most used medium in the area. Just confronting the website of several Russian PSCs with the leading Chinese counterparts, it is possible to spot several differences. The Chinese key points are related to the provision of service as static guards and VIP protection while the Russians advertise a more kinetic approach underlining how companies such as RSB have a great practical battle and command and control experience.

In Central Asia, Moscow might be willing to oversee security operations under the aegis of the Collective Security Treaty Organization (CSTO), while the regional economic sphere of influence belongs to Beijing. However, while Russia is showing the latest military hardware and tactical capabilities in the Syrian conflict, it is doubtful that the Russian Federation Armed Forces are going to re-enter hot areas in Central and South Asia, such as Afghanistan. In this regard, the growing Chinese economic predominance in Central and South Asia and the new power vacuum might force China to become an 'unwilling' security provider in the regional security arena. At the same time, the role of PSCs in Russia is evolving as fast as their Chinese counterparts. In this respect, Deputy Prime Minister Rogozin, besides being the open opposition to the Russian Ministry of Defence, suggested that the state would have to support the role of Russian PSCs within a new framework of law, without repeating the scandals related to the Viktor Bout[20] case. The 'Lord of War'[21] Viktor Bout epitomized how the former intelligence and military contacts derived from the demise of the Red Army have being turned into a profitable corporation, providing illegal arms trade and support to armed militia in Africa and allegedly to terrorist organizations.

The Russian PSCs' focus is related to the capabilities to provide services in high-risk areas, where the contractors could be involved in combat operations. While the Chinese PSCs provide a possibility to provide defensive service, mainly to the Chinese corporations investing abroad, in the Russian case the posture is clearly more aggressive. Foremost, the PSCs' websites include different language versions ranging from English to French and Arabic, tending to address them as private military corporation (PMC) instead of PSC. In comparison, the Chinese PSC websites at most could provide a simplified translation of their Chinese content into English, underlining their lack of interest in the provision of their services to non-Chinese clients. Most of the Chinese PSCs that display effective business communication in English are the ones related to the provision of static security services in mainland China to foreign corporations as the case of Zhong Guo An Bao that guarantees security services to US multinational such as GM or Disney Amusement Park in Shanghai.

> Essentially we do not take part in the armed conflicts like mercenaries and we do not organize consultations for the companies and groups, which

> might be related to the terrorist organizations. We also do not take part in the overthrows of government and other actions, which can break International laws and Conventions.[22]

Besides the aggressive posturing, companies such as RSB claim to have already set in place a set of international certification and cooperation with international organizations such as the UN that could prevent the company to provide illegal or at least questionable use of force.[23]

In comparison to the Western counterparts, the offer of Russian PSC services to China, albeit being late entering the Chinese market, offer several advantages. From a strict Chinese SOEs' point of view, the Russian PSCs provide competitive pricing, personnel with language capabilities that could be essential in several areas covered by the BRI, no links with Western countries that could endanger the business secrecy of the SOEs and, foremost, the 'machismo' that still allures several Chinese PSCs that are more concerned with firepower than risk prevention.

4.3 Kidnapping and Ransom: The Role of Special Insurances

Since the end of the Cold War, several rebel groups set aside their ideological struggle in favour of more lucrative criminal activities ranging from drug production and trafficking to economic kidnapping. Albeit being in the market for decades, the special insurance sector related to kidnap and ransom (K&R) and criminal extortion, started to get notoriety during the kidnapping of several US top corporate managers by the Colombian guerrilla Revolutionary Armed Forces of Colombia (FARC) at the end of the 1990s[24] and more recently during the surge of pirates hijacking along the Somali coast. In 2010 alone, the insurance risk costs related to anti-piracy reached US$200 million in annual premiums (The Economist 2013). Due to the confidentiality that bind the service providers and the clients, and with the exception of the published insurance accounts by the freight companies, the special insurance sector does not provide an easily accessible open-source datasets. Albeit the transparency problem in acquiring the data, it is estimated that during 2015 the overall K&R business was supposed to have surpassed US$500 million in ransoms paid per year.[25] In the areas packed with Chinese personnel, with special reference to Africa, abductions for profit are the norm compared to the abductions for political reasons. Also, extortion along the Chinese construction sites is a common concern, not only for the safety of the Chinese workers but also for the theft of construction materials and equipment and the resulting project loss generated by unexpected delays. Beside North Africa and the Sahel region, the other areas prone with high abduction risks for the Chinese personnel are mainly located in the Afghanistan, Colombia, Venezuela, Mexico, Brazil, Philippines and South East Asia. Compared to the previous century, the business of kidnapping is more driven by religious extremism than political ideologies, but in the end both are motivated by profit rather than principle. Therefore, economic kidnapping is one of the fastest-growing criminal industries (Briggs 2001).

According to Control Risk analysis, the overall risk of kidnapping for ransom in Mainland China is low, though the risk is medium in non-central districts of cities in Guangdong province as well as in remote border areas and the Xinjiang Uighur Autonomous Region. In China, criminals predominantly carry out abductions for financial gain. At the same time, extortion attempts and hostage taking can also occur, particularly in connection with personal or business disputes.[26]

There have been an increase in the number of short-term kidnaps of expatriate managers with International companies in China in the past years. This is driven by the economic slowdown and the need to restructure. There have been a number of cases of workers kidnapping managers as part of the negotiation process.

In the first half of 2015, Asia remained the highest-risk area in the world in terms of kidnapping with the highest-risk countries being India, Afghanistan, Pakistan and the Philippines. China's top management and wealthy individuals are aware of the possible threats to their security especially the one related to K&R, but the real level of risk is still not completely perceived. In this respect, China has already lost several lives due to failed kidnapping but the novelty of the threats is still not weighted with the right concerns. While the employment of close protection personnel, often referred as bodyguard, in Mainland China is more a matter of status symbol than of real necessity, the increase in K&R in Africa and South America is forcing the corporations and the individuals to take more effective actions in preserving their safety.

Several thousand local Chinese PSCs offer their services at provincial and municipal level but just few of them have the capability to provide personnel that could be effectively deployed abroad. One of the main criticisms related to these companies is that the focus is solely on the contractor's combat experience, which in China means decent martial art knowledge. These PSCs and also their clients miss entirely what is needed in order to provide an effective close protection during a travel abroad. There are stories[27] that the so-called bodyguards have been unable to protect their clients abroad because they were not able to obtain a travel visa in time. However, courses to become a bodyguard are mushrooming in China and female bodyguards are among the most requested as a status symbol. While bodyguard schools are located all over the country, the training centres with decent teaching capabilities are mostly located in the capital or offer courses abroad. While the demand for bodyguards is growing in parallel with the Chinese economic growth, the need for more professionalization is a by-product of the security challenges that the Chinese corporations and high-income individuals are facing while travelling outside the country.

While most of the Western multinational groups have some sort of K&R coverage for their staff or even a dedicated security department as part of the company human resources (HR) structure,[28] the Chinese SOEs tend to hire foreign consultants only after the problem has presented itself and the ransom request has already been submitted to headquarters.

Companies such as Control Risks that have fully staffed offices in China are working with Chinese insurers such as Ping An in order to promote a higher level of competencies in the special security field as well as training and services aimed to reduce the risk of a kidnapping. Also, the terrorist attack in Paris and Belgium have ignited fear over a growing number of concerned Chinese CEOs that have started to request ad hoc training and close protection details even during their short-term business trips to the EU. Moreover, special risk intelligence, a product related to security reports and imminent threats in order to avoid to be 'in the wrong place at the wrong time', is still perceived by the Chinese corporations as an unnecessary cost. At the same time, the Chinese insurance market is considered to be a strategic national sector that is heavily regulated in order to protect the local SOEs (PICC, CPIC, China Taiping and Ping An) from the foreign competition. Therefore, the China Insurance Regulatory Commission (CIRC) requirements on foreign insurers impose severe restrictions on overseas insurers eager to enter the Chinese market.

While the threats along the BRI are compounding costs in loss of life, money and project feasibility, it is possible to foresee a faster opening in the field for foreign experts, considering that special risks coverage is not only a common insurance product but a tool to prevent, manage and mitigate crises. The K&R market is a growing niche that involves the expansion of the Chinese economic footprint overseas and the common, often mistaken perception that Chinese tourists and travellers are all very wealthy individuals with an inclination to pay high ransoms on a short notice.

In the BRI the most 'hot areas' for K&R are located along the South Asian path, and in central Africa another hot spot that is not included in the BRI but has come to the attention of the Chinese businessmen is Latin America. Several of the countries that harbour an increased pattern of Chinese investments are areas of high risk. Since the last decade Latin America remains an attractive economic environment for several Chinese SOEs ranging from energy and lately also the tourism and agricultural sectors. Most of the time the SOEs' personnel that approach the area are not aware of the high levels of extortion and violence perpetrated by paramilitary and criminal organizations. One of the most common and threatening forms of extortion is the express kidnapping. This form of kidnapping, quite common in Brazil and Colombia, is related to the abduction and the immediate release, mostly on the same day, after the payment of a limited amount of money compared to the several hundred thousand or million US dollars requested in a long-term abduction. In this respect, Latin America has a historical legacy of kidnapping for ransom as a form of financing for paramilitary and guerrilla groups such as the FARC with hostages that have been abducted and then held in captivity for years. This disgraceful legacy is represented by the six and a half years of kidnapping and confinement of the former senator Ingrid Betancourt.

Currently, the abduction of Chinese nationals is generally perceived in Beijing as a criminal act delinked from political and religious motivations. Nevertheless, the evolution of the China's long-standing non-intervention principle in a contemporary globalized economy does not allow it to escape its obligations and duty as a nascent world power. While China is still holding to the non-intervention principle, the size of the Chinese economic expansion does not allow Beijing to keep relying exclusively on the host countries' security forces to protect Chinese citizens.

The increased political instability that has emerged since the end of the Cold War has also contributed to the growth of kidnapping as a business model. While the demise of large armies allowed a large number of specialized soldiers to fill the ranks of the PSCs, at the same time guerrillas and other armed groups had to find an alternative source of funding in order to continue their struggle. The employment of abduction for ransom has blurred even more the lines between political struggle and criminal violence.

After the collapse of the Soviet Union, funding for ideologically oriented armed groups has been dwindling; thus, kidnapping has become one of the mainstream sources of financing. While the FARC is considered a leading example in the shift from ideological fight to criminal financial gain; criminals operating in areas such as Nigeria as well as several post-Soviet territories are increasing relying on abduction as a cash cow.

Essentially special insurance coverage for K&R is not simply related to the reimbursement of the paid ransom to the company or the family of the individual. But more importantly, special insurance coverage provides access to security consulting services ranging from crisis prevention to support during the abduction process. US companies entering in foreign investment areas deemed to have high abduction risks are used to providing special insurance coverage that can sum up to several hundreds and millions of US dollars[29]; unfortunately on the Chinese side the willingness to pay high insurance premiums is still not yet deemed as essential. The willingness among Chinese SOEs to pay high premiums is toned down by the fact that the risks and threats of kidnapping are not yet perceived as real. Only after a corporate director has been abducted is the company willing to pay a ransom and engage the services of professional negotiators.

A typical K&R insurance policy includes several cost units that range from the rewards offered in bringing the perpetrators to justice to the psychological support to the family victims or even the legal procedures to avoid being sued by the family of the employee in case of death. After abduction has occurred, the insurance policy also could cover the cost of psychological counselling and rehabilitation.

Only a small number of the training activities in Beijing are offered to the local PSCs. These include the role of intelligence to minimize security risks and creation of standard operating procedures to deal with an abduction crisis. As an example, one of the most salient problems faced by several Chinese PSCs advisers located in the Middle East and Africa is the fact that the Chinese engineers maintain a predictable weekly routine that tends to end with a stop at the local alcohol seller and Karaoke outlets with Chinese hostess, in order to provide some distraction from the life inside the working compound. Considering the fact that most of the construction areas are located in Muslim countries, the workers' lack of cultural sensibility in public consumption of alcohol could lead to further problems. Therefore, complacent local drivers familiar with daily fixed routines increase the opportunities for criminals to abduct Chinese workers. Chinese prisoners' value on the criminal kidnapping market increases on daily basis. International specialists based in China observe that Chinese corporations, especially those that have recently commenced operations in South America, are unaware of the level of violence that they are going to face. Once the abduction process has started, especially in the form of 'express kidnapping', Chinese corporations tend to overpay the requested ransom in order to avoid the negotiation process. This attitude will only increase the financial demands from criminal gangs and could also lead to the payment to the wrong criminal group that could insert themselves in the ransom negotiation.

The novelty of the problem, which is going to hurt Chinese companies, will probably force the establishment of crisis management protocols that will be required by the Chinese State Insurance Companies prior to insuring Chinese outbound investments. Prior to the disbursement of preferential grants or lines of credit for projects in excess of US$10 million, the NRDC requires a risk and security assessment. The company that requests authorization to construct infrastructure in a dangerous area has to provide an accurate security analysis that companies such as G4S issue in Beijing or Control Risks in Shanghai. Besides being a good start, the mandatory security analysis is just a preliminary step required to understand what real security means. Unfortunately, the cost of such an assessment is generally perceived by the contracting company as just an additional burden required to receive a preferential line of credit. Chinese insurance experts from companies such as Ping An began to realize the importance of this business niche that is going to provide important profit along the BRI. Other insurance providers such as China Taiping Insurance are testing the waters.

A snapshot of the high-level threat in the African Sahel is presented in the reports of the ongoing K&R in the area just in the month of April 2016. In Mali, where China has already paid a high blood toll with the killing of three top SOEs officers, the risk of kidnap for foreigners is still high. Since 2012, with the central government progressive deterioration, militias and extremists have inserted themselves into the power vacuum. Extremists such as the Ansar Dine group, which has been active in terrorist attacks in Mali and in the border area with Burkina Faso, consider the abduction of locals and foreign nationals as a significant source of profit. On 16 April 2016, four employees of the International Committee of the Red Cross (ICRC) were kidnapped in northeast Mali in the Kidal region. Once again the Islamist group Ansar Dine, which claimed responsibility for the abductions, demanded the release of jihadists previously captured by the French forces. French troops deployed in Sahel are a part of Operation Barkhane,[30] which is intended to stabilize the area and protect the local and international communities. A side effect of hunting for individuals suspected of having links with Islamist militants has generated the hostility within the local population. Therefore, increased protests against the foreign troops led to acts of violence and several deaths. The insecurity among Chinese workers in the area is due to a high threat level.

In Nigeria, employees of natural resources companies remain preferential targets for kidnappers. On 16 April 2016, a Nigerian National Petroleum Corporation (NNPC) technician was kidnapped followed by three employees of the National Iron Ore Mining Company (NIOMCO), who were abducted two days later. On 22 April, a high-level kidnapping was perpetrated against the permanent secretary of the Osun State Ministry of Finance while he and his team were returning from a joint World Bank-EU reform meeting in Abuja. During the entire month of April, several policemen, state officials and university personnel were kidnapped for ransom by extremists and criminal gangs organized by tribal groups such as the Fulani herdsmen. On 5 April, in the southern part of Nigeria a group of gangsters attacked a convoy that resulted in the abduction of a Lebanese construction worker and the killing of a security guard. While displaying cruelty and acts of violence during their kidnapping operations in the southern part of the country, these activities are more related to economic gains via illegal means than they are to extremist militants moved by religious ideology. The ransom requested by the gangsters is in the range of US$50,000 compared to the millions requested by the extremists. Also in Nigeria the abduction of local political figures and their relatives is quite common. In addition, the kidnapping threat for the foreseeable future is considered high all over the country. Also abductions carried out by extremist groups such as Boko Haram[31] are aimed at both locals and foreign nationals. For example, the mass abduction of 276 schoolgirls in 2014 is still an unresolved tragedy.

While the trend of piracy and hijacking diminished in 2016 compared to the previous year, the phenomenon has not been completely extirpated in area around the Gulf of Guinea. Just during April 2016, three hijackings that occurred off the Nigerian coast resulted in the abduction of a dozen crewmembers belonging to the vessels *Mt Puli*, the *Cma Cgm Turquoise* and the *Armada Tuah*.

Additionally, in Somalia piracy remains a major source of income for the local population. In April 2016, more than 50 foreign crewmen were abducted. The lack of local security and the absence of a central power able to quell the criminal phenomenon have led to the creation of inland safe havens that allow the pirates to detain foreign nationals without the need to continuously move them to different hiding places in fear of being detected.

Nevertheless, the decreasing number of kidnappings along the Somali-Kenyan border is probably attributable to fewer foreigners in the area than to a more efficient security prevention. While international anti-pirate efforts have led to a decrease in the number of incidents, the K&R threat is still at a high level due to the presence on land of well-organized criminal gangs and armed extremist groups. In this case, the infamous Al-Shabaab[32] terrorist group possesses the goal and capability to easily shift the base of their operations between Somalia and Kenya in search of high-value targets.

Moving from Africa to South and Central Asia, the month of April 2016 in Afghanistan has witnessed the kidnapping of international aid workers such as Katherine Jane Wilson in Jalalabad province, a dozen of anti-land mineworkers from the international NGO HALO in Heart province and two Bangladeshi nationals in Kunduz city who belonged to an international NGO. The surge in militant abduction activity is claimed by the Afghani Taliban as a source of income to support the struggle. Also the border between Afghanistan and Pakistan provides a permeable area to move abductees. In addition, other areas of Pakistan such as those around the city of Karachi or the tribal area of Waziristan are safe havens where kidnapped foreigners may be held due to the protection of local extremist organizations or a complacent police force.

Despite the increase in bilateral cooperation among China and the Philippines, the Abu Sayyaf Group[33] increased the number of kidnapped hostages. In addition, wealthy Chinese tourists are increasingly being targeted. On 25 April 2016, the terrorist group beheaded John Ridsdel a 68-year-old Canadian tourist who had previously been abducted for a ransom of US$20 million.

China has two primary means to independently respond to kidnappings abroad: the PLA Special Forces and private security firms. For these options to be viable, they must have both the capability and the will to use force in overseas operations. Unfortunately for China, neither option fully meets these criteria (Houpt 2012).

4.4 China PSCs and the Terror Nexus

On 25 July 2016, Al Qaeda chief Ayman al-Zawahiri broadcast an audio interview[34] inciting jihadists to increase hunting for Western hostages in order to create further bargaining chips in exchange for jailed fighters. The threat is not reserved for Westerners alone. According to Duchatel:

> International terrorism has emerged in recent years as a direct threat to Chinese nationals living overseas. As China's footprint becomes increasingly global its exposure to the risk of terror attacks has increased too. (Duchatel 2016)

From the 1990s' Beijing bus bombings, the failed plane hijacking and the futile attempt to detonate a car bomb in Tiananmen Square in the heart of the Chinese capital, radicalized Uighur Muslims have increased their threats inside and outside Mainland China. On 1 March 2015, eight Uighurs conducted an orchestrated suicide attack, stabbing to death 29 innocent bystanders that were commuting at the Kunming train station. Following the Kunming attack several others actions have involved the use of knives and improvised weaponry. The increase in scope and size in radicalized Uighurs attacks are thwarting Beijing plans to stabilize the western province of Xinjiang. The 30 August 2015 bombing of the Chinese diplomatic mission in Kirghizstan (Xin Hua 2016b) marked a shift from the terrorist threats inside Mainland China to attacks on Chinese interests abroad.

Since 2017, the modus operandi of the radicalized Uighurs has changed due to the number of veteran jihadists who are returning after training and combat experience in Afghanistan, Iraq and in Syria (Page 2016).

Looming extremist threats, ranging from the self proclaimed Islamic State (IS) call for Jihad to independent Uighurs in Xinjiang increased Beijing's requirement to escalate the numbers and sophistication of its own counter-terrorism personnel. Since 2001, China enlarged its counter-terrorism efforts with the creation of dedicated departments reaching the grassroots levels, from the national public security agencies down to the municipal level. In this respect, the lack of specialists (China Daily 2016) has prompted Beijing to improve the training and the capabilities of antiterrorism units to prevent and mitigate the extremist menace. While all the training is committed 'in house', Israeli and other foreign specialist trainers are not uncommon guests in the Chinese public security training structures. While mainland areas such as Xinjiang are going to experience an increase in public security personnel with counter-terrorism capabilities, it is not feasible to imagine Chinese PSCs deployed inside the country against extremists. While some municipalities have used PSCs personnel as front-line personnel during street protests, in order to avoid direct contact with uniformed officials, it is not foreseeable to expect local PSCs to face organized riots instead of angry mobs of evicted citizens. On the other side, in the international context it could be possible to witness the employment of the cooperation of trained counter-terrorist PSCs in support of the Chinese forces or in cooperation with the hosting country's security personnel. In the recent white paper on the Middle East, Beijing expressed that upon the invitation of the hosting country Chinese military personnel could be sent abroad to counter extremist threats. Further example of extra-territorial activities by the PAP is given by the hunt for the killers of Chinese sailors in the Mekong River. On 5 October 2011, drug traffickers attacked two Chinese cargo ships on the Thai side of the Mekong River's notorious 'Golden Triangle'. The attack culminated with the slaughtering of 13 crew members. Few months later, the gangsters were arrested in Laos and brought to China for trial and execution. Beijing's main argument on the extradition was based on the fact that the crime occurred on ships waving Chinese flags.[35]

Therefore, international cooperation among security and counter-terrorism practitioners is posed to increase not only in the private sector but also in the public as the Chinese Ministry of Public Security that has started to promote personnel exchanges, overseas training and judicial cooperation with Interpol.

According to a report issued by the New America think tank in July 2016,[36] more than a hundred of Uighur Muslims from Xingjian have joined IS. The numbers are still quite limited, but according to the Chinese sources, they are destined to increase substantially. While Xinjiang is considered by Beijing to be a hotbed for insurgents and terrorist attacks in China,[37] the rebellious province is also a cornerstone of the BRI. While the world is focused on IS' presence in Syria and Iraq, the 'black caliphate' is also posed to threaten China the BRI and the mainland. The growing presence in Afghanistan and in Central Asia is a threat to China's effort to stabilize the Xinjiang Uygur region in the West.

In 2015, an IS video in the Chinese language, which was a call to arms for Chinese Muslims, was addressed not only to Uighurs but also to the Chinese Hui minority. The Hui, often considered 'Muslims with Chinese characteristics', are a Chinese minority of more than ten million that are not historically attracted to holy wars; but in various times in Chinese history the Hui have been subject to tight security controls and even pogroms. While Uighurs are ethnically and culturally closer to the Central Asian's Turkic populations, the Hui are linked to the Chinese Han majority ethnic group. The IS call for Jihad in China and the increased use of political violence to attain greater domestic autonomy is posing a growing economic and security threat for Beijing. According to Campbell:

> the reservoir of people who are disenfranchised and alienated from the Chinese state is increasing. (Campbell 2016)

Since the bombing of the Chinese embassy in Kirgizstan, IS' eastward pivot to Central Asia is on a direct collision course with the Chinese march towards the West.

While the US-led Western coalition in Afghanistan is shifting from a 'boots on the ground' strategy to improving the local Afghan National Army's combat capabilities, PLA and PAP presence on the Tajik border is duly noticed.

Since July 2014, Abu Bakr al-Baghdadi, the former leader of IS, called for Chinese Muslims in Xinjiang to pledged allegiance to him. The IS appeals for jihad are related to a global terrorist threat to China by approximately 20 million Chinese Sunni Muslims. A more geographically defined threat pattern is found in several organizations that are interested in Xingjian's independence from China. Afghan, Russian and American security responses have underlined how traditional strategies and tactics no longer apply to a fast-changing asymmetrical scenario. The Afghanistan jihadist threat of spreading instability in China is too often overestimated, while the drug trade,[38] as a source of illegal financing for local terrorist activities, is—unfortunately—too often neglected (Arduino 2015). On the one hand, the mature Chinese PSCs could be able to provide not only local security but also synergies in information gathering against the spread of extremism. On the other hand, it is imperative to take into consideration how the actions of several international PSCs have increased the host countries' distrust in employing foreign security personnel. Since the abuse and the killings of local civilians by several international PSCs during the Iraq conflicts, the so-called Blackwater syndrome has led to the ban of international private military forces in several countries such as Afghanistan and Ethiopia. Specifically, in the Afghan context, Chinese SOEs have to rely on several layers of protection guaranteed by local tribal militia and the Afghan national army, while the PLA ensures the safety of Chinese diplomatic personnel.[39] While Afghan's new law on PSCs formally forbids the employment of foreign-armed personnel, at the same time Chinese law forbids Chinese citizens from going abroad to carry weapons. Nevertheless, the framework of law still gives space to Chinese PSCs that could be employed as a bridge between local security forces and Chinese enterprises in need of risk and crisis management, security planning and basic training for personnel that are going to be sent to work in potentially dangerous areas. In this respect, the new Chinese anti-terror law,[40] for the first time, allows the PLA to conduct anti-terror operations abroad with the consent of the host country. Therefore, the presence in loco of Chinese PSC could increase mission awareness and threat assessments. Also, the evolution of the Chinese PSC could also promote intelligence sharing and increased joint capabilities with Chinese diplomatic missions and future overseas bases such as the one in Djibouti.

In addition, the increase of security forces devoted to the prevention of extremist attacks from abroad is focused in the Xinjiang autonomous province. The area is the main platform for the BRI Eurasian land bridge that is crossed by oil and gas pipelines and the planned railways and highways that link China with the neighbouring countries and the European terminus. The province border areas are riddled by extremist attempts to thwart Beijing BRI plans.

According to the Xinhua News Agency (Xinhua 2016), a new wave of attacks in Xinjiang has increased security threats. One salient example is the bombing of the Moyu County's Communist Party building on 28 December 2016. The assailants, described by the Ministry of Public Security as ethnic Uighurs, attacked the Chinese officers with knives and detonated an explosive device that killed two people. This renewed extremist surge is forcing the Chinese macro-cities to adopt new policies concerning the security of the urban population and to address terrorist threats. For example, the trend in cities such as Shanghai is to develop a new framework for urban security and crisis management with an increased focus on homegrown extremist threats. The high-level forum 'Public Security and Crises Management in the Internet Era'[41] illustrates how the megacities like Shanghai are facing severe challenges of emergency and crisis management. The forum presented new challenges in the transformation of urban governance and socio-economic reform focusing on the prevention of public events such as threats, cyber risks and emergency rescue in highly populated areas. Similar meetings all over China and Beijing have been hosted in the same year, which have focused on the protection of the BRI with the main Chinese PSCs and the former Blackwater CEO Erick Prince as guests. In this case, several Western scholars consider the Chinese approach in fighting international terrorism to have become increasingly militarized. Therefore, the role of well-managed and reasonably monitored PSCs is going to be pivotal in avoiding military escalations.

4.5 Catching Tigers and Flies: The Hunt for Corrupt Chinese Overseas

According to the official statistics released by the Communist Party of China Central Commission for Discipline Inspection, from 2014 to the end of 2016, 2442 Chinese citizens who escaped overseas to avoid criminal charges have been repatriated. The slogan that resembles the Chinese Communist Party's rhetoric of the Cultural Revolution 'Catching the Tigers and Flies' well reflects Beijing's commitment to crack down on corruption, bringing to justice both high-ranking executives (tigers) and the low-ranking officials (flies).[42]

The anti-corruption campaign overseas has been unleashed in order to repatriate Chinese fugitives who had fled the country in an attempt to escape with the embezzled sums. The figures released present a clear picture of the volume of money that has been transferred abroad by illegal means and the profile of the perpetrators. Almost 15% of the accused are government officials, who have been captured in over 70 countries with a total sum of US$1.2 billion of illegal assets.

The number of criminals captured and returned to the mainland showcases not only the Chinese capabilities to track them down but also the diplomatic capacity in dealing with the legal systems of more than 70 countries. During the last months of 2016, there was also an increase of those who have returned voluntarily in order to face a more lenient punishment compared to that administered after the capture, as in the case of Yang Xiuzhu, one of the top ten fugitives who had been on the run for a decade.

The hunt for the corruptors and the corrupted is already showcasing Beijing's increased cooperation with Interpol and the police and legal systems of countries that host the criminals. At the same time, due to the high volume of criminal cases that involve Ponzi schemes and the embezzlement of several million US dollars, a rising number of Chinese PSCs on the mainland that offer credit recovery are fine-tuning their international capabilities to track the fraudsters and to recover embezzled or stolen funds. While Israel and Anglo-Saxon security companies are the preferred source of training and cooperation for conventional Chinese PSCs aiming to the international market, in the case of commercial fraud the predominant source of cooperation is with Singaporean consulting companies. The Singaporean companies not only provide a solid financial background but also have the language and cross-cultural capabilities to cooperate with Chinese PSCs.

Notes

1. Xinua 'Belt and Road Initiative to embrace greater achievements' Shanghai Daily (Thursday 29 September) Belt and Road Initiative to embrace greater achievements' *By the end of June (2106 ndr) China has signed bilateral investment treaties with 104 countries along the belt and road, while its investment in these countries have totalled USD 51.1 billion.*
2. United States Central Command reported in January 2015 that 54,700 private contractors worked for the Defense Department in its areas of responsibility. http://www.acq.osd.mil/log/PS/reports/CENTCOM%20Census%20Reports/5A_January2015.pdf
3. Author's interviews with international PSC operators in China (Beijing, Shanghai 2014–2016).
4. Table 1. Source: Office of the Under Secretary of Defense for Acquisition, Technology and Logistics http://www.acq.osd.mil/dpap/pacc/cc/history.html
5. Bloomberg http://www.bloomberg.com/research/stocks/private/snapshot.asp?privcapid=128162717
6. 'World military spending resumes upward course, says SIPRI' April 5, 2016. https://www.sipri.org/media/press-release/2016/world-military-spending-resumes-upward-course-says-sipri
7. China Daily 'China, Russia to promote military cooperation' http://www.chinadaily.com.cn/china/2016-11/23/content_27472540.htm, 23 November 2016; RT 'Russia-China military ties 'at all-time high,' no threat to other states' https://www.rt.com/news/367880-russia-china-cooperation-stability 23 November 2016.
8. NDRC official website http://en.ndrc.gov.cn/
9. Comment by a former CIA operative specialized on China, during a workshop on Private Security Corporations in Shanghai January 2016.
10. 'PLA analyses recognize that … because of the one-child policy, young people are pampered and may therefore be more psychologically brittle and less capable of handling stress.'

11. 'Guideline by the Central Committee of the Communist Party of China and the State Council for the Deepened Reform of State-Owned Enterprises' Zhonggong Zhongyang, Guowuyuan guanyu Shenhua Guoyou Qiye Gaige de Zhidao Yijian promulgated by Cent. Comm. of CPC & St. Council, Aug. 24, 2015.
12. SIPRI Military expenditure network on China 2015: http://milexdata.sipri.org/; *IHS Jane's Annual Defence Budgets Review* from IHS Inc. 2014: "By 2015, China will spend more than the UK, France and Germany combined (...) in 2015."
13. ICoC, International Code of Conduct, for Private Security Service Providers is an interstate document that applies international humanitarian law and human rights law to PSC. Employed in conflict zones. http://www.icoc-psp.org/
14. The Montreu Document is the result of a joint initiative launched by Switzerland and the International Committee of the Red Cross in 2006.
15. Most common Chinese social media platforms.
16. On 18 May 2016, Chinese Weibo users lit e-candles to commemorate the UN Chinese peace envoy killed in Mali.
17. '.... already-relaxed restrictions on the security forces of gas giant Gazprom and oil pipeline corporation Transneft are to be lifted, allowing them increased access to lethal weapons and rules of engagement for their use. Mark Galeotti 'Russia and "elastic power": will the burgeoning private security industry lead to private military companies, too?' https://inmoscowsshadows.wordpress.com/2013/06/16/russia-and-elastic-power-will-the-burgeoning-private-security-industry-lead-to-private-military-companies-too/
18. The Russian Criminal Code prohibits creating unlawful armed groups, training and supplying mercenaries The Articles 359 punishes for recruitment, training, financing and using mercenaries. The Article 208 punishes for creating unlawful armed groups.
19. RSB Group Military Consulting Company http://rsb-group.org/about
20. 'Viktor Bout, a Russian man known and feared for his leadership role in international weapons trafficking, was sentenced to 25 years in prison, sparing him the life sentence that federal prosecutors in Manhattan had sought.' Noah Rosenberg 'Russian Weapons Trafficker Avoids Getting Life in Prison' NY Times April 5, 2012 http://www.nytimes.com/2012/04/06/nyregion/russian-arms-dealer-is-sentenced-to-25years.html?rref=collection%2Ftimestopic%2FBout%2C%20Viktor&action=click&contentCollection=timestopics&region=stream&module=stream_unit&version=latest&contentPlacement=9&pgtype=collection
21. Bout was reputed to have present-day Russian intelligence connections, and his legend inspired the 2005 film 'Lord of War'. Ibidem.

22. '*The actions of the company's stuff are not assailant, but restrictive; it allows arranging preventive actions. These actions are needed for supporting main armed forces of the country, according to the general command.*
Private Military Company RSB-Group (Russian Security Systems) was founded by a professional military man, reserve officer of the Russian Border Service. He has a great practical battle and command experience gained on the Tajik-Afghan border. The company's activities are strictly carried out according to the Russian Laws and also according to the Laws of the countries, where we protect the interests of the Russian companies.' RBS website http://rsb-group.org/about
23. RSB-Group works according to the following legislative frames:
UNO Security Council Resolution N 1816;
UNO Security Council Resolution N 1838;
UNO United Nations Convention on the Law of the Sea (Art. 105)
Charter of the UNO (Art. 51)
Code of conduct of the International Red Cross and Red Crescent Movement.
24. 'In the year 2000, Colombia was a country paralyzed by the threat of kidnapping. Guerrilla groups like the Revolutionary Armed Forces of Colombia (FARC) and the smaller National Liberation Army (ELN) set up roadblocks on major highways and kidnapped travellers en masse. Others were targeted for their political beliefs or their wealth, while some merely happened to be in the wrong place at the wrong time. In 2000, 3572 people were reported kidnapped. Nobody knows how many cases were never reported.' Kyra Gurney 'Behind Colombia's Dramatic Fall in Kidnappings' January 13, 2015 http://www.insightcrime.org/news-analysis/behind-colombia-dramatic-fall-in-kidnappings
25. According to Hiscox Group conservative estimate, more than US$500 million a year goes to criminal gang of kidnappers, mostly in South America.
26. Interview with Control Risk Shanghai office September 2016.
27. Author interview with EU Visa Section Consular Officials in Shanghai May 2015.
28. Leading companies in providing K&S special insurances, intelligence and support services are the already-mentioned Hiscocx and Control Risks as well as Integro, Olive Group, NYA International, Aegis and, Seacurus and Terra Firma.
29. 'A lone businessman in Iraq might pay a premium of $3000–6000, while shipping firms have to fork over several million a year to cover large fleets in dangerous areas. All that meant that a market worth about $250 m in 2006 doubled in size by 2011.' The Economist 'Kidnap and ransom insurance

I'm a client ... Get me out of here' June 27, 2013 http://www.economist.com/blogs/schumpeter/2013/06/kidnap-and-ransom-insurance

30. 'The French strategy in Sahel aims to ensure that the partner states acquire the capacity to ensure their safety autonomously. It is based on a global approach (policy, security and development) whose military component is carried by Operation Barkhane, Conducted by the French army. Launched on 1 August 2014, this operation is based on a logic of partnership with the main countries of the Sahel-Saharan Band (BSS). Its priority is to promote the appropriation by the G5 Sahel partner countries of the fight against armed groups (GAT), on the whole of the Sahel-Saharan Band (BSS).This logic of partnership structures the relations maintained by Barkhane with the others forces involved in the stabilization process in Mali: MINUSMA, EUTM Mali and Armed Forces of Mali (FAMa).' Ministere de la Defense 'Operation Barkhane', December 2016 http://www.defense.gouv.fr/operations/sahel/dossier-de-presentation-de-l-operation-barkhane/operation-barkhane
31. Boko Haram was founded in 2002 when Mohammad Yusuf opened a religious complex with an Islamic school in Maiduguri, Nigeria, which attracted students from poor Muslim families across the country. Mapping Militant Organisation Stanford University http://web.stanford.edu/group/mappingmilitants/cgibin/groups/view/553?highlight=boko+haram
32. 'Al Shabaab, meaning "The Youth" in Arabic, is the largest militant organization fighting to oust the Somalian government.' Mapping Militant Organisation Stanford University http://web.stanford.edu/group/mappingmilitants/cgi-bin/groups/view/61
33. The Abu Sayyaf Group (ASG) is an Islamic separatist organization based in the southern Philippines. It seeks an independent Islamic state for the Filipino Muslim minority, known as the Moro people, who live primarily in the Philippines' Mindanao region. The ASG has carried out several high-profile assassinations and bombings in pursuit of its goal, developing a reputation as the most violent Islamic separatist group in the Philippines. While many of the ASG's activities centre on Mindanao and the Sulu Archipelago in the south, where the Moros are concentrated, the ASG also engages less frequently in terrorist acts in the Filipino capital of Manila. http://web.stanford.edu/group/mappingmilitants/cgi-bin/groups/view/152
34. Reuters 'Al Qaeda chief urges kidnappings of Westerners for prisoner swaps: SITE' July 24, 2016 http://www.reuters.com/article/us-pakistan-alqaeda-idUSKCN1040U1
35. 'I think an important message that this case sends is that it shows the determination of China and the governments of relevant countries to work hard together to combat cross-border crime,' Hua Chunying spokesman for

China's foreign ministry said. 'China parades foreign Mekong killers before execution' BBC March 1, 2013 http://www.bbc.co.uk/news/world-asia-china-21625905

36. https://na-production.s3.amazonaws.com/documents/ISIS-Files.pdf
37. 'According to information from various sources, including security officers from Iraq's Kurdish region, Syria and Lebanon, around 300 Chinese extremists are fighting with IS in Iraq and Syria.' 'Turkey's ambiguous policies help terrorists join IS jihadist group' Qiu Yongzheng, Global December 15, 2014 http://www.globaltimes.cn/content/896765.shtml
38. In 2013, according to estimates of the United Nations Office on Drugs and Crime (UNODC), the Afghan-cultivated land devoted to drug production reached more than 200,000 hectares, During late 2015, IS forces seized the southern part of the Nangarharn province, in order to seize a part of the billion-dollar profits derived from the drug business and to control a strategic area near the Pakistani border in the contested Durand line.
39. Discussion with China Institutes of Contemporary International Relations CICIR think tank on May 2015.
40. 'China's new counter-terrorism law has made it legal for the People's Liberation Army (PLA) to participate in counterterror missions overseas. The PLA and the country's armed police forces may carry out such operations with the approval from the Central Military Commission. Public security and national security authorities may also send personnel overseas for counter-terrorism missions, with the approval from the State Council and agreements from concerned countries.' Xinhua 'China passes anti-terror law' December 28, 2015 http://www.globaltimes.cn/content/960826.shtml
41. Organized by the Shanghai Public Relations Association Shanghai on 27 November 2016.
42. China File Infographics on China's Anti-corruption Campaign https://www.chinafile.com/infographics/visualizing-chinas-anti-corruption-campaign

References

Arduino, Alessandro. 2015. Chinese Private Security: A New Paradigm for Private Military and Counter-Terrorism? *Counter Terrorist Magazine*.

Barabanov, Mikhail, Vasiliy Kashin, and Konstantin Makienko. 2012. *Shooting Star China's Military Machine in the 21st Century*. Minneapolis: East View Press.

Briggs, Rachel. 2001. *The Kidnapping Business*. London: The Foreign Policy Centre.

Brooks, Doug. 2002. *Private Military Service Providers: Africa's Welcome Pariahs*. http://www.hoosier84.com/02-00africaswelcomepariahs.pdf. Accessed December 19, 2009.

Campbell, Charlie. 2016. Uighur Extremists Joining ISIS Poses a Security and Economic Headache for China's Xi Jinping. *Time*, July 21. http://time.com/4416585/isis-islamic-state-china-xinjiang-uighur-xi-jinping/. Accessed 2017.

China Daily. 2016. Chinese Public Security University Trains Anti-Terror Specialists. *China Daily*, March 25.

Duchatel, Mathieu. 2016. Terror Overseas: Understanding China's Evolving Counter-Terror Strategy. *European Council on International Relations, ECFR*, December.

Farley, Robert. 2015. Chinese Defense Innovation. Industrial Espionage May Help China's Military-Industrial Complex, But It Will Still Need to Harness Its Private Sector. *The Diplomat*, January 27. Accessed 2016.

Fontanka. 2016. Вагнер в Кремле. *fontanka.ru*. December 12. http://www.fontanka.ru/2016/12/12/064/?utm_source=novapress … Accessed 2017.

Gallagher, Frank, and John M. Del Vecchio. 2014. *The Bremer Detail: Protecting the Most Threatened Man in the World*. Danbury, CT: Charlie Foxtrot Books.

Gleijeses, Piero. 2002. *Conflicting Missions Havana, Washington, and Africa, 1959–1976*. Chapel Hill: University of North Carolina Press.

Global Times. 2015. A Private Dilemma. Chinese Security Companies Struggle to Find Footing Overseas. *China Global Times*, April 21. Accessed 2016.

Gostev, Aleksandr, and Robert Coalson. 2016. Russia's Paramilitary Mercenaries Emerge from the Shadows. *Radio Free Europe Radio Liberty*, December. http://www.rferl.org/a/russia-paramilitary-mercenaries-emerge-from-the-shadows-syria-ukraine/28180321.htm. Accessed 2017.

Hager, Emily B., and Mark Mazzetti. 2015. Emirates Secretly Sends Colombian Mercenaries to Yemen Fight. *New York Times*, November 25. http://www.nytimes.com/2015/11/26/world/middleeast/emirates-secretly-sends-colombian-mercenaries-to-fight-in-yemen.html?_r=0. Accessed 2017.

Houpt, Daniel. 2012. Assessing China's Response Options to Kidnappings Abroad. *Jamestown China Brief*, May 11. https://jamestown.org/program/assessing-chinas-response-options-to-kidnappings-abroad/. Accessed 2016.

Kramer, Daniel. 2007. Does History Repeat Itself? A Comparative Analysis of Private Military Entities. In *Private Military and Security Companies. Chances, Problems, Pitfalls and Prospects*, ed. Gerhard Kümmel and Thomas Jäger. Wiesbaden: VS Verlag.

Lague, David, and Charlie Zhu. 2012. Insight: China Builds Its Own Military-Industrial Complex. *Reuters*, September 16. http://www.reuters.com/article/us-china-defence-idUSBRE88F0GM20120916. Accessed 2016.

Mazzetti, Mark, and Emily B. Hager. 2011. Secret Desert Force Set Up by Blackwater's Founder. *New York Times*. May 14. http://www.nytimes.com/2011/05/15/world/middleeast/15prince.html. Accessed 2016.

McFate, Sean. 2014. *The Modern Mercenary: Private Armies and What They Mean for World Order*. Oxford: Oxford University Press.

Moore, Mark. 1995. *Creating Public Value*. Cambridge, MA: Harvard University Press.

Page, Jeremy. 2016. Over 100 Chinese Fighters Have Joined Islamic State in Syria Studies come as China Seeks West's Cooperation on Counterterrorism, but Cast Doubt on Some of Beijing's Assertions. *Wall Street Journal*, July 27. http://www.wsj.com/articles/china-terror-claims-bolstered-by-new-evidence-1469435872. Accessed 2017.

Rayment, Sean. 2005. Trophy' Video Exposes Private Security Contractors Shooting Up Iraqi Drivers. *The Telegraph*, November 27. http://www.telegraph.co.uk/news/worldnews/middleeast/iraq/1504161/Trophy-video-exposes-private-security-contractors-shooting-up-Iraqi-. Accessed 2016.

Siebels, Dirk. 2014. International Standards for the Private Security Industry. *RUSI Journal* 159 (5, October).

Spear, Joanna. 2006. *Market Forces. The Political Economy of Private Military Companies*. FAFO.

State Council Information Office of the People's Republic of China. 2015. China's Military Strategy. *SCIO*, May. http://www.scio.gov.cn/zfbps/gfbps/Document/1435340/1435340.htm. Accessed 2016.

Tatlow, Didi Kirsten. 2015. Chinese Debate Proper Response to Hostage's Killing. *The New York Times*, November 19. https://sinosphere.blogs.nytimes.com/2015/11/19/china-hostage-islamic-state-fan-jinghui/?_r=0. Accessed 2017.

The Economist. 2013. Kidnap and Ransom Insurance. I'm a Client … Get Me Out of Here. *The Economist*, July 27. http://www.economist.com/blogs/schumpeter/2013/06/kidnap-and-ransom-insurance. Accessed 2015.

Worcester, Maxim. 2014. Putin's Proxy Warfare Strategy. *ISPSW Strategy Series: Focus on Defense and International Security*, Issue No. 282 August.

Xin Hua. 2016a. China Appreciates Cambodia's Support on S. China Sea. *Xinhua Net*, August 8. http://news.xinhuanet.com/english/2016-08/01/c_135553379.htm. Accessed 2017.

———. 2016b. China Strongly Condemns Car Bombing Near Chinese Embassy in Kyrgyzstan. *Xinhua Net*, August 30. http://news.xinhuanet.com/english/2016-08/30/c_135645520.htm. Accessed 2016.

Xinhua. 2016. Two Dead in Wednesday's Terrorist Attack in Xinjiang: Police. *Xinhua Net*, December 29. http://news.xinhuanet.com/english/2016-12/29/c_135941561.htm. Accessed 2017.

Zenko, Micah. 2015. The Unknown Soldiers of Afghanistan and Iraq. *Foreign Policy*, May 29. http://foreignpolicy.com/2015/05/29/the-new-unknown-soldiers-of-afghanistan-and-iraq/. Accessed 2017.

CHAPTER 5

Conclusion

Abstract The post–Cold War security vacuum is characterized by an increasing demand for mercenaries and private military services. The evolution of the private security company (PSC) sector has been driven by demand from international corporations to protect their natural resources, extraction projects and broader activities, globally.

The American private military security company Backwater's aggressive tactics in Iraq and Afghanistan have earned critique and scorn; yet, at the same time, they have been praised by the government officers and civilians they were escorting. Beijing's security circle is actively discussing the compatibility of the Blackwater model with China's security needs. The evolution of Chinese PSCs from the mainland's simple model of static guards to modern international security providers is already ongoing.

Keywords BRI • PSC • Security with 'Chinese characteristics' • BRI security • BRI threats

© The Author(s) 2018
A. Arduino, *China's Private Army*,
https://doi.org/10.1007/978-981-10-7215-4_5

5.1 Chinese Private Security Companies: Just Another Blackwater?

In Iraq, the postwar business boom is not oil. It is security. James Hider, *The Times*

The post–Cold War liberal world order is fading, and the global political and economic system is entering uncharted territories.

Uncertainty is driving up multinational corporation operational costs while driving down foreign direct investment (FDI) profits. The Belt and Road Initiative (BRI) map, which is linking new trade routes, promotes China's win-win narrative for a connected and integrated global market. Usually when China is involved in a win-win narrative, it means that China aims to win twice. In this case the BRI's overambitious projects, if successful, could not only sustain the export of Chinese industrial overcapacity but also support the global economic system by creating mutual benefits. The new borders traced along the BRI are fluid, and the private sector is going to have a strategic role in defending them.

In its involvement in Iraq and Afghanistan following the September 11 attacks, the US government chose to rely heavily on contractors to provide security services. In 2007, the US Army had 160,000 soldiers in Iraq, supported by some 180,000 private employees working for 630 contractors from more than 100 nations. According to the 'Cost of War'[1] report, the number of US troops who died fighting in both wars surpassed 6800 by the beginning of 2015. During the same year, the number of contractors killed surpassed 6900. The Government Accountability Office (GAO) and Department of Defence (DOD) do not provide an accurate account on deceased non-uniformed personnel; therefore, it is possible to presume that the figure does not reflect the gravity of the problem.

At the height of the Iraq and Afghanistan conflicts, several private security companies (PSCs) profited from billions of US dollar contracts with the US government, including Halliburton (services), DynCorp (counterinsurgency—security) and Parsons (infrastructure building). A few others had to share less lucrative contracts, as well as bear the full blame for the indiscriminate use of force against civilians. At the peak of the conflicts, Defence Secretary Donald Rumsfeld expanded the privatization of the US government's military and legal support and granted the contractors immunity from the jurisdiction of local law. The contractors' immunity, normally granted by the law of war to an army's personnel, created a particular anomaly in the private market for force, and thus increased the risk of abuse.[2]

At the peak of the stabilization efforts, the ratio of government personnel to contractors reached 1 to 1.3 in favour of the contractors. With less fanfare, the number of contractors employed by the United Kingdom was three times that of British soldiers on the ground.

The US PSC Blackwater managed to attract most of the critical commentary and a high-profile brand name; the company is now commonly associated with the adjective 'infamous'.[3] Misconduct by Blackwater operatives reached its highest point during the 'Baghdad Bloody Sunday' tragedy. In September 2007, a convoy of Blackwater armoured vehicles entered Baghdad's crowded Nisour Square. Blackwater's contractors, perceiving a threat, opened fire on civilian vehicles, killing 17 people and wounding more than 20 others. In October 2007, relatives of the Nisour Square victims sued Blackwater in US federal court for extrajudicial killings and war crimes (The New Your Times 2014). Seven years later, a jury in the Federal District Court found that the deaths of 17 Iraqis in the shooting were the result of a criminal act, not an act of self-defence against a threat.

Blackwater's aggressive tactics have earned critique and scorn, yet at the same time have been praised by the government officers and civilians they were escorting. During the above-mentioned court hearings, it was underlined several times how the reconstruction efforts could not have been implemented and civilian agencies in Iraq could not have functioned without Blackwater's support. After all, the pitch that 'Blackwater never lost a client during its work' still has a positive echo in Beijing security apparatus corridors.

While Blackwater PSC personnel performed acts of bravery in support of marine counterparts in distress (Prince 2008), acts of violence and reported blatant infractions of Iraqi law caused lasting damage to the effort to win the hearts and the minds of the Iraqi population. The first congressional investigation into the Nisour killing concluded that under US law independent contractors are not accountable for their actions. However, a subsequent FBI investigation found that several of the Nisour Square shootings were unjustified. Numerous accounts of Blackwater's unprovoked violence against civilians and the lack of punishment, as in a previous case involving the killing of an Iraqi official's bodyguard by a drunk Blackwater contractor, endangered US military relations with the Iraqi government and populace. At the same time, the overall actions of

PSCs increased the negative perception of the US counter-insurgency efforts as well as increased the probability of retaliatory attacks.

During the Iraq conflict and the following counter-insurgency stabilization effort, the overall private market for force was inundated with cash from government contracts. Blackwater's rapid expansion, which led to the employment of thousands of contractors from various countries, underlines the possible risks to substantial growth of Chinese PSCs. As already mentioned in the Phoenix report, overly aggressive expansion will not promote stable growth of the Chinese private security market. Without the proper control and auditing systems in place, unprofessional PSC personnel, potentially even personnel with former criminal records, could fill the growing ranks of PSCs and generate more problems than solutions. Unaccountable contractors operating in legal limbo could not only endanger civilians, but also perpetrate criminal acts such as promoting illegal weapons trade. In relation to this kind of nefarious behaviour, Blackwater was fined US$2 million by the US government for export control violations.[4]

Since the demise of Blackwater in Baghdad, the compelling demand for security in Iraq forced the DOD to select the next PSC in line. While a change in the role of private security was expected, the urgency just let the main clients to opt for another actor in the market for force. Despite the Iraq government's ban on all international PSCs, the next private military company to take over Blackwater's (already rebranded Xe at that time) contract in Iraq was the US PSC Triple Canopy. Founded in 2003 in Chicago by former US Special Forces operators, Triple Canopy[5] became one of the leading security providers in Iraq with DynCorp and Blackwater. Triple Canopy's offices around the globe provide kidnapping and ransom (K&R) protection and even business intelligence. At the same time, the company's global footprint allowed for recruiting South American and Central African private security officers as stationary guard in Afghanistan and Iraq at a fraction of the North American counterparts. Interviews with former Western operators[6] in Iraq confirmed than numerous Xe/Blackwater contractors migrated to Triple Canopy as soon as the State Department contract was terminated. Several Blackwater operators migrated to Triple Canopy as quickly as the following day.

The US government's commission subsequently scrutinized Triple Canopy over the quality of the 'Third World country' nationals under their contract. The commission findings underlined several faults including the employment of untrained Ugandan nationals to protect the US embassy. By 2014, Triple Canopy had been subsequently absorbed by the Constellis Group, which owns Academi (former Xe/Blackwater).

> US contingency contractors, opportunistic labor brokers, and international criminal organizations have taken advantage of the easy flow of people, money, goods, and services to capitalize on this source of revenue and profit. Their actions bring discredit to the United States and act as a barrier to building good diplomatic relations.[7]

While contractors are often seen as disposable, in this specific case the direct association with the DOD and the State Department did not provide any of deniability to the US government. The backfire triggered by Blackwater and PSCs in general profoundly damaged the war effort. Compared to their US counterparts, Russian PSCs granted a broader range of deniability to the Russian Federation in the initial involvement in the Syrian conflict. Today, the deniability offered by the Chinese PSC is still debatable. Chinese PSC personnel previously linked to the armed forces is already casting suspicions over government-hidden agendas, or even parallel security structures,[8] that are operating abroad under the aegis of Beijing's security apparatus. While the reality is still far removed from the imagination, the vision of undercover People's Liberation Army (PLA) officials disguised as PSCs will linger for a long time.

Erik Prince succeeded in rocketing his company from a shooting range to an army worth billions in the span of years. At the apex of the company's expansion, Blackwater's contractors could even rely on their own armed air support. After 9/11, Blackwater's scope expanded exponentially, coupled with the company's revenues. The private security services company enlarged its client portfolio to include State Department overseas protection, and even the CIA. While the initial revenue in 1998 was in the range of US$400,000, by 2006, the total revenue surpassed US$1 billion in no-bid contracts with the US State Department. Chinese PSCs aim for the same growth trend, quoting the Blackwater model as successful and profitable one, considering the fact that despite fines and investigations, the company has continued to win contracts from the State Department and the CIA.[9] At the same time, several Chinese academics in the Beijing's security circle are already underlining the incompatibility of the Blackwater model with China's security needs. Blackwater's high profile does not fit well with Deng Xiaoping's catch phrase 'keeping a low profile while hiding its own ability' (tao guang yang hui),[10] which formed the strategies of generations of Chinese communist party officials and the PLA.

Other international PSCs that have longer histories than the newcomer Blackwater, such as DynCorp or Triple canopy, kept their names known strictly inside PSC and military circles. Though Blackwater's high-visibility approach attracted prospective clients, it also drew international media attention. The bravado characterizing the company's statements after the Nisour Square killings and other incidents resurfaced historical disdain for 'mercenarism'. Images of white mercenaries fighting in Africa with impunity evoked the collective memory of war profiteers and the business of violence. Chinese PSC's footprint is still far from this model, and Beijing is already well aware of the potential negative consequences that would emerge if notoriety was achieved. In the recent past, several incidents in Africa and Central Asia have surfaced involving Chinese managers firing their locally acquired weapons on throngs of local workers, or even getting killed during working condition disputes.[11] Nevertheless, the lure of the Blackwater machismo remains present in Beijing security circles.

Blackwater has been repeatedly sold, and had its name changed from XE to Academi. Meanwhile, Mr Prince has managed to train a new PSC to support Saudi military capabilities. The engagement between Mr Prince and China began with participation in the HK company Frontier Service Group (FSG), which has offices in Hong Kong and Beijing and is supported by Chinese financial group CITIC. Until December 2016, the company's business vision advertised on their website was related to the provision of advanced logistical services with special respect to Sudan and other African states. FSG analysts and Mr Prince himself have participated in Chinese think tank conferences regarding the role of private security in protecting the BRI. At the end of 2016, the FSG website statement changed abruptly, underlining how the company is ready to support the training of unarmed Chinese security personnel along the BRI. At the same time, the personal figure of Mr Prince is back in the spotlight thanks to his sister Betsy DeVos being nominated as the new education secretary in President Donald Trump's government (Scahil 2017). The question about Mr Prince's role in China is related to the perception of alleged transfer of military expertise to support the PLA increase its capabilities (The Washington Times 2016).

Training camps for Chinese unarmed PSC personnel are not new to Beijing, as well as the offer of armed training courses outside of China. The FSG's proposal to open two training camps in Mainland China reported by several media sources is a common business trend that several international and local PSC have tried to exploit since 2014. The FSG website statement includes the provinces of Yunnan and Xinjiang as the two preferential areas to operate training structures in China. At the same time, the choice of Xinjiang could raise some eyebrows as the area is at the centre of the main Chinese counter-terrorist efforts against the perceived menace of Uighur separatists. Further, the province of Yunnan is at the frontline of China's struggle to contain suspected terrorist routes from Xinjiang to Thailand, and the province remains central to Beijing's battle against the drug trade sourced to China's south-eastern borders.

FSG's claims as recent as last year of merely being a logistics company are contradicted by the release of a new business model, reflecting to Mr Prince's principal skill set. According to FSG's press release, in order to 'help clients take advantage of China's One Belt One Road initiative FSG will provide training, communications, risk mitigation, risk assessments, information gathering, medevac and joint operations centres that coordinate security, logistics and aviation.' A reasonable question is whether the next change in its business model will include FSG's direct involvement in Beijing's armed security efforts.

Mr Prince's return in the 'White House grace' is hinted by his commentary in the *Wall Street Journal* (Prince 2017) in which a five-point recipe is given to address the Afghan conundrum. Mr Prince exhorts President Trump to avoid 'too many cooks in one kitchen', nominating a viceroy that will centralize all the operational decisions.

> It's time for President Trump to fix our approach to Afghanistan in five ways. First, he should consolidate authority in Afghanistan with one person: an American viceroy who would lead all U.S. government and coalition efforts—including command, budget, policy, promotion and contracting—and report directly to the president. (Prince 2017)

While Mr Prince's analysis of Afghanistan failures denotes a deep understanding of the previous and ongoing situation on the ground, the proposed solution of a modern East Indian company private military security approach discounts too many variables. Nevertheless, if the American viceroy card is not going to be played, the allure of imperial mandate from Beijing Forbidden City is still in the air.

5.2 New Wars, New Businesses

In the market for force, an operator's main concern is the fact that they are paid to put themselves in the line of fire on a daily basis. That said, the rationale for the high salaries contractors demand is related to this daily risk. Machiavelli's chief critique of mercenaries relates to their attitude of avoiding putting themselves at risk, and even switching sides if the tide of battle turns. Cyber warfare and remote warfare by drones, mostly armed unmanned aerial vehicles (UAVs) are already changing this trend. The advent of the Internet has simplified the call for arms in the market for force, with websites[12] like www.shooterjobs.com offering pay checks in the range of US$150,000 per year for qualified contractors. New warfare paradigms bring a contractor's dreams to fruition, which is to provide security services from their couch at home. Several corporations are already bidding to complement the security umbrella of Chinese worker sites with aerial drone surveillance. The offers of supporting security services range from small drones to professional blimps and long-range aerial remote surveillance.[13]

PSCs flying armed drones for the army, or ensuring the safety of the perimeter of oilfields in unstable areas, have become commonplace since the expanded use and off-the-shelf availability of remote-controlled vehicles. The private market for aerial drones is largely related to aerial photography, agriculture and real estate aerial survey or utilities inspection. Nevertheless, security surveillance is a rising opportunity in the market for force. From the military side, the privatization of drone warfare is already in effect, and drone video analysis, piloting and communication are steadily shifting to the private sector. As with the case of the revival of PSCs, the US armed forces spearheaded the employment of private corporations with UAV capabilities. A growing number of reports indicate that the US armed forces are using a increasing number of contractors to operate reconnaissance and even to carry out lethal drone attacks. 'Drone mercenaries' are already creating uneasiness in military circles with civilians inserted into the kill order chain of command. During the Afghanistan conflict, the German army has taken the lead in the peacekeeping mission. More than 15,000 flying hours using Israeli-made drones[14] have been outsourced to the private Canadian company Cassidian.[15]

> Drones fired more weapons than conventional warplanes for the first time in Afghanistan last year and the ratio is rising, previously unreported U.S. Air

> Force data show, underlining how reliant the military has become on unmanned aircraft. (Smith 2016)

Nevertheless, the role of intelligence gathering and surveillance conducted by private firms is still questionable and floats in legal limbo. The surveillance function itself, albeit not directly linked to the discharge of air-to-ground missiles from the UAV, can endanger the population under surveillance, leading to intelligence misuse and collateral damage.

While the US reliance on PSCs in Iraq and Afghanistan has enlarged the military industrial demand for UAV contractors, from the Chinese side, the growing production of civilian UAV by Chinese industries is facilitating the local companies' ability to provide drone services.

The PSCs with added drone capabilities are already carving a niche in the market for force. Chinese state-owned enterprises' (SOEs) drone requirements along the BRI range from threat scouting to search and rescue operations during natural disasters. Furthermore, the market efficiency guaranteed by the PSC with UAV capabilities is related to pay per use. The SOEs, or their main PSCs, do not have to bear the cost of maintaining a drone fleet and the related pilots and analysts during idle time, as this responsibility rests in the hands of the niche drone PSC. As UAV technology is becoming more sophisticated, ubiquitous and affordable, it is possible to foresee a faster development of Chinese PSCs with remote drones having air, land and maritime capabilities.

5.3 China's Private Army: From Rule-Taker to Rule-Maker

> Build walls and bridges: effective security management is a spectrum with walls, alarms and guards at one end, and conversation at the other. Realistically most projects require a mixture of physical security and dialogue to solve security problems. (Humphreys 2017)

The role of China as an emerging power has already transformed the country's position in the regulation of international trade from rule-taker to rule-maker.

That uncertainty and lack of clear and enforceable international guidelines from any international organization allow China to assert valuable influence over the growing PSC sector. The size of the market for force with Chinese characteristics is posed to influence international codes of conduct that are already following a shift from the West to the East. However, the US leading role in the employment of PSCs will not fade overnight. While US boots on the ground in the Middle East and South Asia are decreasing, the new remote warfare is increasing the demand for contractors. Nevertheless, the new PSC legal frameworks have to take into consideration the new role and responsibilities that China asserts as a rising power, as well as the mature and leading role that the United States has reached in the market for force. Though Chinese economic power and infrastructure building are unmatched, the complete maturity of the state and private security sector is not foreseeable in the near future.

Despite the economic decline and self-insulation, European Union (EU) regulatory power and policy guidelines are still functional to China. Multilateral cooperation amongst China, the United States, the EU and the Russian Federation in creating oversight of the market for force not only will provide effective policy tools and a controlling mechanism for Chinese PSCs, but also could curb the perception that China has been too assertive.

The current literature on the market for force presents PSCs as *conditio sine qua non* for the US Army to preserve the momentum in different operational fields (Schwartz 2009). At the same time, other foreign governments as well as international organizations including the United Nations (UN) increasingly rely on PSCs in dangerous areas.

The use of contractors with armed capabilities has raised a number of concerns that will affect how China will act in the adoption of PSCs. The range of issues that have emerged from the US experience are not yet on the list of Beijing's immediate concerns, but incidents along the BRI will force a sudden reality check. Beijing's proper PSC oversight is essential to promote accountability, transparency and avoidance of incidents involving excessive use of force. At the same time, it is important to stress an often-overlooked factor: the business nature of the PSC engagement. While the BRI is attracting a growing number of PSCs, some areas with insignificant budgets will receive insufficient security coverage. Chinese PSC competition will be fierce in areas of financial importance, starting with the energy SOEs' oil and gas fields, followed by railroad and highway construction plans, down to lower-level financial projects. The same issue especially applies to Chinese private PSCs, scrapping for the crumbs of BRI macro projects. Often these small- to medium-level enterprises are adventuring outside Chinese national borders, following the SOEs as subcontractors. Their budget for private security as well as risk management and threat assessment are minimal to non-existent. Here, it remains to be seen whether Beijing's willingness to provide security will be adequate, or if the Ministry of Foreign Affairs (MFA) will be left alone to act once a crisis occurs.

Beijing, starting with the two latest national and international initiatives—the 2015 US House of Representatives National Defence Authorization Act (NDAA) and the International Code of Conduct Association (ICoCa)—has the chance to investigate and employ recent findings and policy suggestions without reinventing the wheel. The NDAA aims to improve the US defence department's PSC management and oversight in Africa, the Middle East and South Asia. The policy findings need a suitable cultural adaptation to Chinese effective requirements, but the data remain invaluable and will be beneficial in avoiding costly mistakes in the future. At the same time, the ICoCa's broader international reach, including the International Committee of the Red Cross in Switzerland, offers to China the means to fill the gap from national regulations and international ones. A broader integration with the UN as well as a regional platform such as the Shanghai Cooperation Organization (SCO) will also prove beneficial in promoting efficiency and constraining PSC bad behaviour and other negative impacts.

Strengthening legal compliance, overview and regulation is an important step in making China a rule-maker and not a passive actor in the market for force.

The new framework of law that China is going to introduce in the market to force regulation needs to avoid 'regulatory capture' by interest groups. China's growing influence in the PSC sector results in China regulating itself. If the gamekeeper becomes the poacher, the regulatory agency could be 'captured' by the national and international organizations that are supposed to be the controlled.

A concomitant step relates to profound transformations that Beijing needs to enact in perception and risk management. Most of the analysis carried out on the BRI security needs is increasing in sophistication, but remains riddled with internal faults, and is considered to be risk static. A correct appraisal of risk and threats demands continuous monitoring of the evolution of risk.

Chinese projects along the BRI are subject to the evolution of risk over time, and several of the risk variables will be triggered by the progression of the Chinese projects. In Central Asian countries such as Kazakhstan, present political risks relate to President Nursultan Nazarbayev, the ageing 'father of the nation'. Sudden government changes in the region could spread instability, and a new government could create sudden, negative pressure on the Chinese presence. Further, political risk includes a dichotomy between the central government and the regional governments. The competition for Chinese resources could drag Beijing into local political infighting, endangering Chinese workers and increasing stress on the project's financial viability.

In the China Pakistan Economic Corridor (CPEC) example mentioned in Chap. 3, competition has emerged for Chinese resource allocation. Focus on locality must even extend down to the village level. In each of the three national, regional and local levels, the dynamic ignited by the sudden influx of Yuan creates winners and losers.

On a broader political level, aligning with China could promote political careers and gather government support, which could ignite competition in neighbouring countries that perceive or are concerned with China's increasing economic power and influence. For example, China's support of Islamabad has provoked India's ire. India's perception of Chinese containment of the Indian Ocean is already changing the regional security dynamics. At the regional level, risk evolution is intertwined with local political and social dynamics, which can mistakenly be minimized or underestimated during the project-planning phase. Nevertheless, most of BRI infrastructure projects involve land declaration of imminent domain. The appropriation enacted by central governments usually ends in public protest and resentment towards Chinese corporations. At the local level, constant monitoring of risk evolution, though essential, is often underestimated. Chinese SOEs subcontracting with local workers and suppliers for daily necessities favours a fraction of the local villagers, which increases resentment amongst those left empty-handed during the 'Chinese gold rush'. At the same time, Chinese workers' behaviour, like the consumption of alcohol in Muslim countries, could result in local strife, potentially manifesting in protests and delaying a project's schedule.

5.4 Is China's Dream Going to Be a Safe Dream?

A lot of ink has already been spilled defining what a PSC is, and whether security privatization is a solution, or just another part of the problem. Despite different historical and cultural settings, the role of lances for hire constantly shifts between indispensable and disposable. Chinese PSCs, which will also surge and decline, will not deviate from the traditional pattern.

The post–Cold War security vacuum is characterized by an increasing demand for mercenaries and private military services. The evolution of the PSC sector has been driven by demand from international corporations' demand to protect their natural resources extraction projects and broader activities globally.

Moreover, governments that are unable to stabilize their country without external armed support also increase the demand for private security. During the 1990s, a successive transformation of the market for force was characterized by industrialized states employing private contractors in order to privatize the army's non-core functions in various war theatres. The aftermath of 9/11 signalled the peak in contracting private forces to support the fight against terrorism. Currently, the rise of the BRI in 2013, spearheaded by the Chinese SOEs, induces novel demands for a new market for force. New actors include a spectrum of contractors that range from international PSCs with a corporate structure, more similar to a multinational corporation than to the private militaries before the 1990s, to an increasing number of Chinese PSCs with global ambitions. The growth of the Chinese PSCs resonates with the controversial role played by international PSCs in US-led conflicts.

The natural selection process to develop mature Chinese PSCs has been ignited by the BRI security requirements. At the same time, the protection of Chinese infrastructure and nationals abroad is only the start of what could become a larger trend in the privatization of force with 'Chinese characteristics'.

Albeit marginalized in the first wave of the Chinese FDI in 'hot areas', the role of the Chinese PSCs is poised to increase in unison with threats directed at Chinese overseas direct interests. The evolution of Chinese PSCs from the mainland's simple model of static guards to modern international security providers is already ongoing. The mix of terrorist threats, criminal extortions and political violence and the increase in Chinese SOE security budgets are already catalysing the changes. At the same time, a more mature domestic insurance security sector is going to support the increase of professionalism in the Chinese market for force.

These new soldiers of fortune are now part of complex corporate structures that are supporting Chinese enterprises across the BRI by providing security for Chinese workers and infrastructure. A first glance at today's private security market, as compared to the involvement of PSCs in the Iraq and Afghanistan conflicts, could lead one to believe that a scaling back in quality and quantity of private security services is in order; however, this is not the case. The BRI 'glocal' need for security in today's global marketplace will supply lucrative contracts and demand sophisticated PSCs capable of intelligence acquisition, risk analysis and crisis management across several countries. PSCs with Chinese characteristics are not at the forefront of the next battlefield, but will rather occupy a niche market between state provision of security and the preservation of Chinese economic interests overseas. The contemporary market for force's main driver, as in all business, is profit, and Beijing is well aware of the potential.

The aforementioned three macro-trends of the privatization of the state monopoly on violence have characterized the last several decades. Moreover, each trend is not to be considered as complete caesura with the past as hybrid forms of mercenaries and private military corporations coexist with the modern PSCs. From the 1970s to the beginning of the new millennium, an evolution in the private provision of force has generated a steady shift in the state monopoly on violence towards control by the private sector. One characteristic remains unchanged, however: widespread resentment in the countries where PSCs operate.

China is now imposing the latest set of changes on private security service requirements. Beijing's overseas economic ambitions and the presence of Chinese nationals all over the world, with nearly 200 million students, 600 million overseas Chinese and several million Chinese workers abroad, have brought pressure upon the central government and MFA to protect Chinese overseas interests. Also, Beijing's economic might is shifting from the previous PSC's role as a supporter of armies, to a role in support of SOEs. Nevertheless, lessons from past mistakes in the employment of PSCs can be applied to prevent unnecessary tragedies. A new set of regulations must be implemented, ranging from a Chinese licensing mechanism enforceable nationally, to international monitoring organizations with judiciary and enforcing capabilities, in order to avoid disasters such as 'Baghdad Bloody Sunday'.

While the situation of the Chinese market for force is still informal and in dire need of increased efficiency, it is possible to predict a consolidation of the sector in few years. The severity of the risks along the BRI will promote natural selection among those Chinese PSCs exposed to external threats. A similar example is seen in the Chinese steel sector that grew too rapidly during the 1990s. The high demand for iron and steel by the housing and industrial sectors characterized two decades of China's breakneck gross domestic product (GDP) growth. With the subsequent decline in demand for steel, Beijing forced a comprehensive consolidation of the sector. State-owned groups absorbed smaller steel mills in order to regain efficiency and competitiveness while avoiding overcapacity and dispersion. The selection was not left to the 'hidden hand of the market' but to the central government's five-year economic development plan. A similar demand for PSC consolidation is a current necessity. Consolidation of the Chinese private security market is intended not only to compete with the international PSCs but mostly to provide necessary services that will enable the BRI to deliver promised support to the Chinese 'new normal' economic soft landing. At the moment, the Chinese market for force is a closed one and the competition with international PSCs is not considered the sole catalyst in reforming the sector. Chinese PSCs do not feel their international peers' competitive pressure, as Chinese regulation shields local service providers from any serious external competition.

In the case of a multitude of SOEs, the central government is a single monopolistic client that is not going to allow open and transparent competition, especially when services provided are overlapping with the national security directives. At the same time, international PSCs have the knowledge base and experienced human resources that are going to be contracted by Chinese counterparts. Therefore, cooperation with international PSCs will be tolerated until the craving for the transfer of intellectual capital is satiated.

One immediate risk in the BRI security market is represented by the cheap options provided in several countries by local militias and unprofessional PSCs that offer their services at below-market prices. Only since 2017 have Chinese high-level mainland companies inland started to realize the importance of qualified security companies. The internal market for static security services is a race to the bottom in terms of costs versus service provided that has been damaging the revenues of companies that contract with substandard local PSCs.

Chinese SOEs without the proper security market knowledge and economical evaluation of risk are prone to choose the cheapest available option. The asymmetry in the pricing information is a problem that most of the Chinese SOEs are still unable to appreciate. Focusing solely on the price of security services and not on the quality of the output is still a common mistake among SOEs managers that are already fighting narrow profit margins. This situation is also encouraged by a current lack of detailed regulations and a performance monitoring system. Furthermore, lack of proper capacity screening and feedback to the central government allows dishonest actors to promote themselves as qualified security service providers. In Beijing private security circles, it is not uncommon to meet foreign and Chinese nationals who claim former special forces or intelligence affiliations in order to obtain training contracts or, even worse, to provide international support without the necessary knowledge and capabilities.

The staggering pace of growth of the PSCs in the 1990s raises again interest and concerns over the direction of the US$100–150 billion annual global revenue. Over the last five decades, the privatization of the state monopoly on violence has shifted from the active combatant role to the support of the army and the counter-terrorist effort. In this period of time, PSCs' employment has perpetrated human right abuses, indiscriminate act of violence and illegal arms trade. On the other hand, advocates of PSCs employment stress their role in promoting stability where weak states cannot afford to supply their own security services or economic savings and market efficiencies. Regardless of competing narratives, the provision of private security services along the BRI must take into account past mistakes in order to prevent history from repeating itself.

PSCs with Chinese characteristics focus solely on the security of construction areas, industrial installations and, overall, the BRI's logistical efforts. The degree of violence that Chinese PSCs could employ in response to external threats is still limited and relative to local laws and regulations.

Today, the American way of war has already showcased PSCs' positive and negative outcomes ranging from outsourcing cost savings to long-term damage to strategic efforts. Private soldiering in the new millennium has left unanswered centuries-old questions on how the use of force by non-state actors is appropriate. The BRI security narrative will experience the same problems when the increase of violent threats to Chinese assets is going to blur the line between defensive security and pre-emptive strikes. At the same time, the various stakeholders that are involved in the BRI could deviate or cause deviations from Beijing's blueprint. SOEs with different agendas and Chinese PSCs not aligned with the central government's long-term strategy could ignite unexpected crisis.

The lack of transparency, accountability and separation from established chain of command structure is a current fixture of the private market for force. While it is not a question whether Chinese PSCs will have a foreign policy of their own, their undisputed allegiance to Beijing should not be taken for granted.

Several factors will affect Chinese PSCs' allegiance to Beijing: specifically, the opacity that characterizes Chinese corporate structure and its relationship with SOEs. Take, for instance, the former Chinese public security minister Zhou Yongkang's membership in the so-called Oil Mafia (BBC 2015) and his subsequent demise in a purge during President Xi's fight against corruption. The relationships between PSCs and clients are difficult to trace, and when state secret is involved, it is almost impossible to ascertain responsibilities. Even now, Blackwater's relationship with the CIA as an external service provider is still covered by state secret.

The never-ending story of the legitimacy of the PSC is not going to end with the involvement of China. Nevertheless, the debate over the market for force must strive to impose a strict regulatory and auditing framework that includes multilateral cooperation and enforcement mechanisms. The Chinese 'socialist market' approach could promote real incentives for the best practices, as well as punishment for misconduct. At the same time, when Chinese national interests diverge from international consensus, the regulatory mechanism is going to be under pressure from the main stakeholder.

The mismatch of perception and reality is going to be particularly brutal for those that are underestimating the risks and threats along the BRI.

Notes

1. 'The Costs of War Project is a team of 35 scholars, legal experts, human rights practitioners, and physicians, which began its work in 2011. We use research and a public website to facilitate debate about the costs of the post-9/11 wars in Iraq and Afghanistan, and the related violence in Pakistan and Syria. There are many hidden or unacknowledged costs of the United States' decision to respond to the 9/11 attacks with military force. We aim to foster democratic discussion of these wars by providing the fullest possible account of their human, economic, and political costs, and to foster better informed public policies.' Watson Institute for International and Public Affairs http://watson.brown.edu/costsofwar/costs/human/military/killed
2. Paul L. Bremer, US ambassador to Iraq, employed Blackwater contractors for his close protection and security. 'Under Bremer's orders, the 170 private contractors in Iraq enjoy immunity from prosecution. Iraqis cannot bring charges against them; in fact, Iraqi and U.S. authorities have never put a contractor on trial for a crime.' Jeremy Scahill 'Blackwater. The Rise of the World's Most Powerful Mercenary Army' Nation Books, 2007.

3. Ibidem.
4. 'The violations included illegal weapons exports to Afghanistan, making unauthorized proposals to train troops in South Sudan and providing sniper training for Taiwanese police officers, according to company and government officials familiar with the deal.' James Risen 'Blackwater Reaches Deal on U.S. Export Violations' New York Times, August 20, 2010 http://www.nytimes.com/2010/08/21/world/21blackwater.html
5. 'Triple Canopy offers comprehensive program management solutions to support government agencies and multinational corporations in high risk and complex environments across the globe. Our personnel bring a dynamic combination of expertise and experience to each challenge–delivering long-term, cost-effective programs that are specifically tailored to meet customer needs.' Triple Canopy Company presentation and official website: http://www.triplecanopy.com/about-us/company/
6. Interview with former PSC operator in Iraq that provides training to the Chinese PSCs in Shanghai (May 2014).
7. 'Transforming Wartime Contracting Controlling costs, reducing risks' Final report to Congress Findings and recommendations for legislative and policy changes; Commission on wartime contracting in Iraq and Afghanistan. August 2011,The report is still available online at: https://cybercemetery.unt.edu/archive/cwc/20110929213820/http://www.wartimecontracting.gov/docs/CWC_FinalReport-lowres.pdf
8. 'They and the military are in reality two sides of the same coin.' Charles Clover 'Chinese private security companies go global Beijing's protection industry looks after workers in the most dangerous places' Financial Times February 26, 2017 https://www.ft.com/content/2a1ce1c8-fa7c-11e6-9516-2d969e0d3b65
9. 'In June, the State Department awarded Blackwater a $120 million contract to provide security at its regional offices in Afghanistan, while the C.I.A. renewed the firm's $100 million security contract for its station in Kabul.' James Risen 'Blackwater Reaches Deal on U.S. Export Violations' New York Times, August 20,2010 http://www.nytimes.com/2010/08/21/world/21blackwater.html
10. Tao Guang Yang Hui: 'Xiaoping's proposal, which he reads as meaning "observe calmly, secure our position, cope with affairs calmly, hide our capacities and bide our time, be good at maintaining a low profile, and never claim leadership." But some foreigners read it as advocating deception about China's true strength. Zhao maintains that "keep a low profile" is not a trick, but an expression of a particular approach. Yet other scholars point out that in a classical context, the phrase is used to indicate a strategic ruse. 'Global Times June 15, 2011 http://www.globaltimes.cn/content/661734.shtml
11. 'In 2010, Zambian police charged two Chinese supervisors at the Collum mine after they shot and wounded 13 miners during another pay dispute'

Andrew England 'Zambian strikers kill Chinese supervisor' Financial Time August 5, 2010 https://www.ft.com/content/6967bc22-df24-11e1-b615-00144feab49a

12. shooterjobs.com advertises overseas high-risk contracting jobs to local armed security and law enforcement. 'We don't cover admin jobs, only positions that require former military or law enforcement experience.'
13. Documents on drone reconnaissance and drone security patrolling for Chinese pipeline construction in Ogaden basin, Ethiopia, provided to the author by local PSC, September 2016.
14. Rheinmetall Airborne Systems GmbH, a joint venture by Cassidian and Rheinmetall, will continue to support the German Armed Forces in Afghanistan by providing unmanned airborne reconnaissance services. The Federal Office for Defence Technology and Procurement (BWB) prolonged an existing order to the company to provide the German Armed Forces with Heron 1 ultramodern unmanned reconnaissance aircraft for two more years. The volume of the order prolongation amounts to about €75 million for the period from October 2012 to October 2014. 'German Military in Afghanistan Extend UAV Coverage with Heron' SUAS News July 17, 2012 https://www.suasnews.com/2012/07/german-military-in-afghanistan-extend-uav-coverage-with-heron/
15. 'Cassidian SAS develops and manufactures security solutions and systems. It offers lead systems integration, and value-added products and services, which include air systems (aircraft and unmanned aerial systems), land, naval and joint systems, intelligence and surveillance, cyber security, secure communications, test systems, missiles, services, and support solutions to civil and military customers around the globe. The company offers nationwide security, security of deployed forces, security of critical infrastructure, event security, communications network security, cyber security, and through-life services solutions.' www.cassidian.com

References

BBC. 2015. Profile: China's Fallen Security Chief Zhou Yongkang. *BBC*, October 12. http://www.bbc.com/news/world-asia-china-26349305. Accessed 2016.

Humphreys, Michael. 2017. Seven Ways to Smooth Your Path Along the Silk Road. *Control Risks*, February. https://www.controlrisks.com/en/our-thinking/analysis/seven-ways-to-smooth-your-path-along-the-silk-road. Accessed 2017.

Prince, Eric. 2017. The MacArthur Model for Afghanistan Consolidate Authority into One Person: An American Viceroy Who'd Lead All Coalition Efforts. *Wall Street Journal*, May 31. https://www.wsj.com/articles/the-macarthur-model-for-afghanistan-1496269058. Accessed 2017.

Prince, Erik. 2008. *Civilian Warriors: The Inside Story of Blackwater and the Unsung Heroes of the War on Terror.*
Scahil, Jeremy. 2017. Notorious Mercenary Erik Prince Is Advising Trump from the Shadows. *The Intercept*, January 18. https://theintercept.com/2017/01/17/notorious-mercenary-erik-prince-is-advising-trump-from-the-shadows/. Accessed 2017.
Schwartz, Moshe. 2009. The Department of Defense's Use of Private Security Contractors in Iraq and Afghanistan: Background, Analysis, and Options for Congress. *Senate*, September 29.
Smith, Josh. 2016. Exclusive: Afghan Drone War—Data Show Unmanned Flights Dominate Air Campaign. *Reuters*, April 20. http://www.reuters.com/article/us-afghanistan-drones-exclusive-idUSKCN0XH2UZ
The New York Times. 2014. Blackwater Guards Found Guilty in 2007 Iraq Killings. *The New York Times*, October 23. https://www.nytim such aes.com/2014/10/23/us/blackwater-verdict.html?_r=0. Accessed 2016.
The Washington Times. 2016. Former Blackwater Chief Under Investigation for Deals with China, Libya: Report. *The Washington Times*, March 24. http://www.washingtontimes.com/news/2016/mar/24/erik-prince-former-blackwater-chief-under-investig/. Accessed 2017.

Index[1]

[1] Note: Page numbers followed by 'n' refers to note.

© The Author(s) 2018
A. Arduino, *China's Private Army*,
https://doi.org/10.1007/978-981-10-7215-4

The manufacturer's authorised representative in the EU is Springer Nature Customer Service Centre GmbH, Europaplatz 3, 69115 Heidelberg, Germany. If you have any concerns regarding our products, please contact ProductSafety@springernature.com

Printed and bound by CPI Group (UK) Ltd, Croydon, CR0 4YY
30/09/2026
02225466-0019